# CAN YOU TOP THIS?

"How c'n I write the word 'book' when there's only one 'o' on this silly typewriter?"

# CAN YOU TOP THIS?

BY

"SENATOR" ED FORD

HARRY HERSHFIELD

JOE LAURIE, JR.

CARTOONS & SKETCHES BY THE AUTHORS

BLUE RIBBON BOOKS

GARDEN CITY, NEW YORK

**D**EDICATED, WITH GREAT APPRECIATION AND DEEP HUMILITY, TO OUR PUBLIC WHO DISPLAY TOP INTELLIGENCE AND BRILLIANT JUDGMENT IN MAKING OUR SUCCESS POSSIBLE.

"SENATOR" ED FORD
HARRY HERSHFIELD
JOE LAURIE, JR.

# CONTENTS

# FOREWORD

THE RADIO PROGRAM "Can You Top This?" is the brain child of "Senator" Ed Ford, who not only created, produces, and owns the show, but also appears in it with the noted wits Harry Hershfield, cartoonist, raconteur, and columnist; and Joe Laurie, Jr., pint-size author and comedian.

"Can You Top This?" is an audience-participation show in which the listening audience sends in stories and jokes that are edited and presented by character actor and dialectician Peter Donald in the role of peoples' representative. The three knights of the Clown Table—Laurie, Hershfield, and Ford—then try to top the submitted story with a joke on the same subject.

The person whose joke is presented by Peter Donald automatically receives ten dollars. Each time the three wits fail to top the sent-in joke, the contestant receives five dollars more.

The visible audience is the judge. Its laughter volume is registered on a big laugh meter in full view of the studio audience. It is calibrated from 1 to 1,000.

"Can You Top This?" is unrehearsed and spontaneous. Hershfield, Laurie, and Ford do not know what jokes are to be used until Peter Donald presents them on the air. They have no scripts or notes, but draw solely from a vast repertoire

9

of jokes and humor gathered during their many years in show business.

This book contains some of the jokes, prefaces or "quickies," and Clown Table discussions of "Can You Top This?"

*Thumbnose Sketch of*
"Senator" Ed Ford
*by Joe Laurie, Jr.*

Reprinted from the *Lambs' Script*

A STORK FLYING blind over Brooklyn dropped a tiny package into the home of Mr. and Mrs. Ford. The year, to be exact, was a long time ago. He was not as old as he looked, and still looks it. At the christening he behaved very well, because they practiced for two weeks on him with pails of water. When they dried him, he was labeled Edward. And so that was the beginning of what we now know as "Senator" Ed Ford.

He attended grammar school and high school for a few years, then set out to get an education. He worked in an antique shop (started gathering his jokes there), a machine shop, was a bookkeeper (still owes 6 cents to the Public Library), photographer, sold insurance, worked in a broker's office and finally decided to do art work. He was at the Academy of Fine Arts for a few months, but left there when they started using automatic elevators. He then turned to commercial illustrating. It was about this time he got mixed up with a coal-box harmony quartette. The first job they got was to sing at a funeral. They went there and found that the man wasn't dead yet, and were told to sing until he died. They did it in less than a chorus. Our hero Ed quit the quartette, being outvoted by the three others, and did a cartoon act in clubs, while doing illustrating to make a living on the side. The junk he was carrying was too heavy, so he left it home and started doing a straight talking act in a business suit. The suit did very well, lasting him for a number of years. He got more money for doing less.

He then fell into an after-dinner speaking job at the Republican Club in New York. (In those days the Republicans still spoke.) Warren G. Harding, then a Senator, spoke ahead of our hero, but Ed followed him without much trouble. The toastmaster introduced Ed as follows: "This man is a substitute. I don't know how good he is, but time was short and we had to take what we could get." And in a facetious moment, he said: "I introduce you to SENATOR ED FORD." Thus the "Senator" title was born and it has stuck ever since. Ed has never asked for a recount. Since then he has become a professional athlete of the tongue, or, in simpler words, an after-dinner speaker, and a very good one. He has been on the speaking lists with five Presidents without a casualty. They have all since gone, but the Senator lingers on. He is the poor man's Chauncey Depew.

Then vaudeville called and the Senator brayed back. He has played all the Big Time Vaudeville houses in the East and West for five or six years. He didn't stop any shows, but he did slow up many of them. He also wrote a book entitled *After Dinner Speaking and Other Forms of Insanity*, and to prove it he has nearly the complete edition in his library.

He then entered Radio, was the first guest star on the "La Palina Hour" and was paid off with a cigar which he is still smoking. He wrote, cast, directed, and played in a domestic comedy (which script contained no broken legs, hearts, or bubonic plague) called *The Grummits*, which ran for fifty weeks. He then made one of the first talkie shorts for Warner Brothers, and contributed to much of the "box-office poison." He played one night in *Artists and Models*; he didn't like his spot and quit. The show survived for two years. He then reached the highest spot in show business when he played the Rainbow Room on top of Radio City; he played there twice, for a run of six and seven weeks.

In the art world, he helped the noted Dwight Franklin on the much-talked-of groups "South Street" and "Inauguration of Washington," which are on exhibition at the New York Museum. He also made a wonderful figure of John McGraw, the Napoleon of the Giants, which now occupies a prominent spot at the Cooperstown Baseball Museum.

Our hero has made his home in Southold, Long Island, for over twenty years. It's a very quiet town; even the cats are all indoors by 7 P.M. In his youth, the Senator was a pitcher; "he threw 'em and ducked." He managed the Southold High School Team and they won a pennant; he also managed the Southold Team in the East Long Island League and they, too, won a pennant. So you see he has done his pennants for a living in Southold.

Between after-dinner gassing, he has originated a radio program idea called "Can You Top This?" Harry Hershfield, the noted newspaperman and raconteur, and Joe Laurie, Jr., the pint-size author-comedian, appear on this program with the Senator on station WOR every Wednesday night, and on the N.B.C. network on Saturdays. The program features story telling, belly laughs and wit. Hershfield takes care of half the story telling, Laurie takes care of half the belly laughs, and Ford half the wit.

The Senator most always wears a convalescent grin—he is what every girl fears she will meet on a blind date. He has been married to a lovely lady for nearly thirty-five years; she is just beginning to laugh at him.

Senator Ed Ford is a good Lamb, besides being a nice, humorous, talented, decent, honest, friendly American gentleman. CAN YOU TOP THIS?

*Thumbnose Sketch of*
HARRY HERSHFIELD
*by Joe Laurie, Jr.*
Reprinted from the *Lambs' Script*

CEDAR RAPIDS, IOWA, being in the "corn belt" of America, it was only natural for "a stalk" to deliver a "corny kid" on October 13, 1885, to the parents of Harry Hershfield. It was also natural for them to christen him Harry Hershfield; if you ever look at him, what else would you call him? The baby had dimples all over his face and looked like a golf ball, his father put him to sleep with a mashie, his mother caddied. Today there is a Burma Shave sign on the site where Harry was born.

Although born in Iowa he was "grazed" in Chicago, where

he immigrated to at the age of two. He immediately entered kindergarten, where he flunked in blocks and sand pile. He went further and had the distinction of being the only kid in the sixth grade that the teacher called Mister. He graduated grammar school at the age of fourteen, which must have been a gag on his teacher's part. He then went to the Frank Holmes School of Illustration, where he studied art and soon knew all the arteries (they had live models). In no time Harry was able to draw on his father. By now he figured he was illiterate enough to enter the newspaper business.

Harry got a job on the Chicago *Daily News* doing sport cartoons, a comic strip called "Homeless Hector," was a retoucher and sketch artist. His main assignment was making X's on pictures showing where crimes were committed. All this for six bucks a week. He was jack of all trades but there was practically no jack in any of them. He also did chalk-plate drawings for the *Drover's Journal*, a stockyard official organ. They claim his drawings started the famous Stock Yard odors. In 1906 Harry covered the Republican National Convention, which attracted the attention of Charles de Young of the San Francisco *Chronicle*, who hired him for that paper. He was now rising from nothing to something worse.

All men are created equal but Harry became a cartoonist. He covered sports and the theater, tired of it and arranged for Bob Ripley to replace him while he went back to Chicago to work on the Chicago *American*. Arthur Brisbane hired him for the New York *Evening Journal*, and when Harry arrived in New York he looked for the press gate in the subway. Harry was hired to do sport cartoons but he saw what a bum he was, against a guy like TAD, so he started his famous "Desperate Desmond" strip which ran for four years. He then started his successful "Abe Kabibble" cartoon which ran for many years. He also ran a column called "Broadway Unlimited" for the same paper. After a contractual mixup he joined the *Graphic* as a columnist, called his column "If I'm Wrong, Sue Me!" The *Graphic* folded but our hero didn't. He went to the *Herald Tribune* with a Sunday comic called "Meyer the Buyer," which was practically a Republican version of Abe Kabibble. He was then hired by the *Mirror* to revive the indestructible Abe Kabibble. He was struggling hard to be a failure but it didn't work. He became a radio commentator, doing a nightly sting (spelled correctly) called "One Man's Opinion," in which he reviewed the theater. He then started his *Sunday Mirror* column "My Week," which at this writing is still running. As a side line to his newspaper work he appeared on the Milton Berle radio program called "If You Heard This One, Stop Me." They did. Up to now his name meant one thing in radio. Shut it Off! He then joined the "Can You Top This?" radio program with those two sterling artists, Senator Ford and Joe Laurie, Jr., and regained all his prestige. As a "warm-up" and proving grounds for his gags he is on a Sunday program for a cheese sponsor.

In between all these radio and newspaper jobs Harry did many things. He played Hammerstein's years ago with a cartoon act. If the billboard would be turned upside down he would be the headliner. From Hammerstein's he went to London, England. We don't know if the offer came from America or England. He then threw his chalk talk away and played vaudeville as a story teller, and a great one. He took a flyer in Hollywood as Animation Editor for M.G.M. and as a script writer for the Warner Brothers. He was so popular in Hollywood, when he arrived there they wanted to give him a farewell dinner. And speaking about dinners, Harry is one of the foremost after- and before-dinner speakers in the country.

In 1936 he spoke at 226 dinners. He was a semi-pro, being paid half the time. He has introduced and been photographed with some of the greatest personalities in the world. He is a B.A. of Gab. He speaks with his hands; when he has a sore throat he doesn't have to gargle, he just rinses his hands. He also has written books like *Les Misérables*, but livelier. His novel *Super-City* was grand and his joke books *Ye Old Salami Shoppe* and *Now I'll Tell One* are still selling. You can't reckon sale of such books by numbers; you reckon them by the ton. You can get them in any drugstore with aspirin.

Harry is the co-standard bearer, with another great Lamb, of the McCosker-Hershfield Cardiac Foundation, a glorious organization that does splendid work. Harry is a Mason, Elk, Modern Woodman, B'nai Brith, Saints and Sinners, Dutch Treat, Illustrators, Friar and a Lamb. He also has been president for twenty-nine years of the Cheese Club; they figure it's cheaper to keep him in office than to buy him a present on retiring. He was adopted by the Hopi Indians, and named "La-Ti-Yo," which means "Silver Fox." He has had a dozen offers from I. J. Fox just to sit in the window.

For recreation Harry likes fishing and auction sales, where he buys up abandoned furniture and oil paintings. He also likes singing on key, but can't! He is stage struck, will play anybody's benefit. He can tell Irish, Italian, Swede, German and French stories all in the same dialect. He loves to be photographed, and photographs like a Rand-McNally map. His love and avocation is Ecclesiastical Art. In his office he has many stained windows. That's what he gets for having an office near pigeons. Harry has so many fine points you can use him for a hat rack. As a toastmaster he invented inflation in the field of compliment dispensing. His accent is a mixture of N.B.C. Oxford and Early Bronx. The only guy who ever brushed him off is the guy in the men's room. He quotes himself to add spice to his conversation. When he asks a question you have a feeling he is setting a trap. If you want to know how really great a man he is, you must ask him to tell you himself.

He adds up into a grand guy. I like him for his humor and humanity. His wit and mirth give him a passport to the thoughts and hearts of everybody he meets. He is an Aristocrat in sentiment and a Democrat in opinion. He is a missionary of laughter and in his heart he has a sacred something we call sympathy. He is a human human. In the words of Kipling: "He has walked with Kings but never lost the common touch." What I'm trying to say is: "I'm just wild about Harry." Aren't we all?

## Thumbnose Sketch of
## JOE LAURIE, JR.

### by "Senator" Ed Ford and Harry Hershfield
### (With no apologies)

JOE LAURIE, JR., was born in New York, at Market and Madison Streets—only the city and streets refused to change their names.

He went to grammar school, according to witnesses (nine truant officers). "I never graduated," he cries, when faced with printed matter. He feels that if the sign language is good enough for the Indians, it's good enough for him. But that doesn't stop him from writing letters to himself—what's more, he steams open the letters before reading, to feel that somebody else is involved.

He left grammar school because it wouldn't look good in his biography later if he hadn't started in first as a newsboy. Here was Horatio Alger—with the emphasis on the hooray. He was so honest a newsboy that he paid for one of his own newspapers rather than peek at the want ads for a real job.

To meet the onslaughts of a competitive business world, he had stationery printed with "Joe Laurie, Jr." at the masthead. Even in those days he bought or swiped wholesale. That's why, with so much stationery still on hand, even now in his old age he still calls himself "Junior." At this moment Mr. Laurie is trapped somewhere in Shakespeare's immortal line: "If age but could and youth but knew." Let's hear his side of the lie.

Claims he held about eighty jobs (that ain't "holding," brother—that ain't even in the neighborhood of touching them). Ran the gamut, from messenger to "stick man" in dice games—some of the toss-ins being exercise boy for Newcastle racing stables, florist, copy boy for Dow, Jones & Co.—Sulka & Co.—shirtwaist factory—office boy for Street & Smith—petticoat factory—bookbinders—drugstore—water boy for harvest hands (just wants to show he read *Gunga Din*)—lawyer's office, dentist, diamond setter, jewelry store—made garters (before the rubber shortage), etc. Ladies and gentlemen, have you ever seen such a preparatory course for a guy who wasn't going to get any work as an actor? Up to then, his life was as intelligent as a P.S. on a telegram. No person could be engaged in so many endeavors unless he was envious of the people who owned the places. He just couldn't take it —except those stamps that stuck to his sleeve on his way out of an office. He wrote something on his coat and mailed it— the answer getting him his first appearance on the stage at a Firemen's Benefit at Greenlawn, L. I., with Aileen Bronson, in an act written by themselves. (The immaterial involved is not a thing of the past—it will live forever in everything he has written before or since.) From that Firemen's Benefit on, it was strictly catch-as-catch-can!

Aileen and he were featured in *Over the Top*, a musical comedy with Ed Wynn, T. Roy Barnes and Justine Johnstone. Joe wrote ten scenes for this show and gave Fred Astaire his first speaking part, which is the reason Fred became a dancer! Later, "Junior" was starred in the successful musical comedies *Gingham Girl* and *Plain Jane*. Following astrology, he was also starred in *Great Little Guy* (which he is but we hate to admit it) and *Weather Clear, Track Fast*, which were both "legit" plays. He was also featured in *Swing Your Lady*, which had nothing whatsoever to do with his domestic life or Sing Sing!

Then came the Dawn!

Joe got the bug and started to produce. His first effort was *Memory Lane*, which boasted the biggest cast of old-timers ever assembled outside of an oxygen tent. This play didn't lay an egg; it laid a cake with twenty eggs in it! Then Joe went back to writing because, after all, he had to eat—not much, but something. He wrote over one hundred vaudeville acts, and acted as a play doctor shooting beaucoup adrenalin into many a sick show (to hear him tell it!).

The "Joe Grim" of the show business, he persisted in writing Skits and Blackouts for Revues, and Eddie Cantor and Al Jolson! Broadway didn't know how to get rid of him! Magazines feared him and in self-defense published many of his articles. He has been with *Variety* for thirteen years now, which proves how unlucky *Variety* is!

Joe has been a guest star on many radio programs. Rudy Vallee had the same problem with him that *Variety* has, but

Rudy was lucky and got rid of him after nine consecutive weeks!

Joe has collaborated on many stage plays with famous writers like Ben Hecht, Gene Fowler, Paul Gerard Smith and many others. The fact of the matter is he's busier than a trap drummer at all times and horns in on everything!

We won't tell you about the many successful pictures he has written and acted in, because this thing is getting to read like the sequel to *Anthony Adverse*—so we'll start to fade.

To all this we can only requote the traveling salesman dialogue: "Guess how much I made last year?" "Half." Like other actors, "he spent in the summer the money he didn't make during the winter." He isn't far removed from Booth, seeing they both suffered. (In fact, we would say that Laurie's "oy" is a little more dramatic.) More data, if you will. Has served as toastmaster and speaker at most of America's public dinners. Has one son, Joe Bryant Laurie, 3rd—now in the Air Corps. His recreation is pool, collection of vaudeville trivia and comedy library. Collector of dogs and cats, canaries (18) and fish (the latter puts him back into economic security again, if his voice holds out).

In rebuttal to our own inventory, we claim: Joe Laurie, Jr., is second to none in contributing to the world much of its gaiety. His trigger-mind repartee is proverbial. His own philosophy is summation enough: "I'm an optimistic futilist. I know everything is the bunk—but very interesting." His friendships are lasting. Those who have passed on have really lived longer than himself—for he always keeps their memories green. There is a definite niche in the records for Joe Laurie, Jr.

P.S. He is no relation to Annie!

# 1
# ART GALLERY

"Who was that lady I saw you with?"
"That was no lady—that was my lunch!"

HAND DRAWN BY JOE LAURIE, JR.

"Now you see why they've got to warn hoodlums."

"Remember, Rome wasn't built in
a day."
"Looks to me like it was."

"This is General Pozzle on his horse. The committee ran out of funds."

MOONIE LIZZIE

SENATOR FORD

"*Reminds me of my wife when she doesn't believe what I'm saying.*"

"Mr. Smith isn't feeling well. He can't come to the office today. This is my wife speaking."

(This is an old joke, hence the old golf togs.)

"*I've got to go home, I have a* stew
*on the stove.*"
    "*Gee!* That *ought to cure him!*"

**HAND DRAWN BY JOE LAURIE, JR.**

# 2

# PREFACES OR QUICKIES

*("Warm-up" Stories and Jokes which
are never scored on the Laugh Meter)*

Little Dorothy was reading the war news.

"Mama," she said, "what do they mean by close quarters?"

"Trying to get twenty-five cents out of your father," answered her mother.                                           FORD

A gun moll saw a handsome guy and wanted to know who he was. Although she asked everyone, no one knew. So, she shot him. The next day she read the papers and found out who he was.                                                       HERSHFIELD

A fellow went to see a Gypsy fortuneteller.

"Let me see your crystal ball," he said. She showed it to him. "You've got two holes in it," he remarked in surprise.

"Yes," she replied. "I go bowling nights."        LAURIE, JR.

Around Christmas time, those street corner Santa Clauses each have a pot with pigeon wire over the top so the kids can't steal the nickels. In other words, so Santa Claus won't be "nickel-less."                                                  FORD

How a German radio war communiqué used to sound:

"The enemy flew planes over the Reich territory. We shot down one hundred Allied planes, but lost four fighters. One of our cities is missing."                                  HERSHFIELD

A fellow down South was sitting on his porch holding a small piece of rope.

"What's that?" asked a stranger.

"That's my weather vane," was the reply.

"How can you tell the weather with that?" inquired the stranger.

35

"When it goes to-and-fro, it's windy. When it's wet—it's raining!"  LAURIE, JR.

A fellow offered to sell a used car very cheaply. "There's not a thing the matter with it," he assured, "the only thing I'd advise you to do if you buy it, is to file the number off the engine."  FORD

A man put his little son on the mantelpiece, then held his arms out and told him to jump into them. As the kid jumped, his father stepped aside. The kid fell on his nose and broke his teeth. "That's to teach you a lesson," he said. "Don't ever trust anybody—not even your Father!"  HERSHFIELD

A woman was running down the street. "Where are you going?" called a neighbor. "I'm going to get a divorce from the grouchiest man in the world," was her reply.

"Go on," sneered the neighbor, "how can you get a divorce from my husband!"  LAURIE, JR.

I know an absent-minded nudist who went out one time, with his clothes on!  FORD

One of Sam Goldwyn's employees became a proud father. "What did you name your son?" inquired Goldwyn.

"John," replied the employee.

"Why did you name him John?" asked Goldwyn. "Every Tom, Dick and Harry is named John!"  HERSHFIELD

As a truck passed by, a draftee saluted. "What did you salute that truck for?" asked the Sergeant.

"On it," explained the draftee, "it said—General Hauling."  LAURIE, JR.

A draftee from the Ozarks was about to take his physical. "Have you any scars on you?" asked the examining doctor.

"No," replied the draftee, "I haven't any scars, but I can give you a cigarette." FORD

An Army aviator was telling about his first night flight. "For the first thousand miles, I was flying blind," he said, "but I sobered up before the trip was over." HERSHFIELD

A kid had the sniffles, which annoyed a woman who was standing next to him. "Listen, young man," she said, "have you got a handkerchief?"

"Yeah," answered the kid, "but my Mother won't let me loan it to anybody." LAURIE, JR.

A bashful chap went into a furniture store. Indicating a piece of furniture, he addressed the attractive blonde saleslady. "What is that?" he asked.

"Highboy," she said.

"I'm fine," he replied, "how are you?" FORD

A goofey guy got into the Army and was put on sentry duty. The Colonel walked up to him. "I'm the Colonel here," he informed. "Whatever I say goes!"

"Oh, you've got a good job," said the goof, "don't louse it up!" HERSHFIELD

Two partners were bemoaning the fact that their tailoring business was terrible. "I wish Gabriel would blow his horn," moaned one.

"Why should Gabriel blow his horn?" asked the other.

"All the dead people will come to life and they'll need clothes!" LAURIE, JR.

Up in my town, a farmer owns a boarding house. One summer, a boarder showed unusual interest in everything rural and asked how long cows should be milked. "The same as short ones," informed the farmer. FORD

A girl wanted to elope with a certain fellow. Her irate father locked her in his room. She took his trousers, escaped through the window, and eloped. The heading in the paper about the incident was—Flees In Papa's Pants! HERSHFIELD

Two fellows were talking about their sweethearts. "What are you going to give your girl for a birthday present?" asked one.

"Book ends," informed the other.

"It's a shame to cut up a whole book just to give her the ends, ain't it?" mused the not-too-bright chap.

LAURIE, JR.

There's no more white-collar class these days, because the laundries can't do up the collars any more! FORD

A cop brought a moron into court. The Judge took one look at him and had his number. "I want to tell you something about the law," he cautioned. "Whatever you say will be held against you."

"You mean," asked the mental delinquent, "anything I say will be held against me?"

"Yes," assured the Judge.

"Rita Hayworth!" gasped the moron. HERSHFIELD

A shapely blonde applied for a job on a girl's baseball team.

"Can you catch?" asked the manager.

"I caught a fellow," she replied.

"Can you run?" was the next question.

"How do you think I caught him?" inquired the blonde.

LAURIE, JR.

A sentimental wife was gazing out of the window watching a gardener burning leaves. She sighed deeply, then called her husband's attention to the scene. "Look, dear," she said, emotionally, "what does that scene remind you of?"

He took a quick gander. "The cigars you gave me for Christmas!" was his blunt reply.

FORD

A couple of morons pooled their bankrolls and bought a little second-hand car. They went driving up the mountains, going around corners and dangerous curves at sixty miles an hour! Finally one moron couldn't stand it any longer. "Every time you go around one of those hairpin bends so fast, I get frightened," he confessed.

"If you get frightened," advised the other, "why don't you do like I do?—I keep my eyes closed!"

HERSHFIELD

A refugee questioned a friend. "Jake," he asked, "what kind of business can I go into? I'd like to invest some money."

"Why don't you write Mrs. Roosevelt?" suggested Jake.

"Who wants partners?" said the refugee.

LAURIE, JR.

A loyal native was talking to a local Quisling in a Norwegian village. "What are you going to do when the Allies win the war?" he asked.

"I'll put on my hat and leave," informed the Quisling.

"But what are you going to put your hat on?" inquired the loyal one.

FORD

A husband and wife were having breakfast. "You know," she said, "that you swore at me in your sleep last night?"

"Who was asleep!" he replied, indignantly.

HERSHFIELD

A moron went to a doctor. "Hey, Doc," he said. "Remember two years ago you cured me of rheumatism?"

"Yes, I remember," answered the doctor.

"You told me to stay away from dampness too, remember?" questioned the moron.

"Yes," said the doctor.

"Is it O. K. to take a bath now?" he asked.    LAURIE, JR.

Will Rogers predicted World War I wouldn't last very long because his brother-in-law joined the Army and he never held a job for over two weeks.

FORD

Do you know how a workman starts a story these days?— "Once upon a time-and-a-half . . ."    HERSHFIELD

A woman went into a haberdashery. "I want to see some ties," she said. The salesman showed her a large assortment. "I'll take this green one," she declared.

"I'd like to make a sale, lady," admitted the honest salesman, "but I don't believe that your husband would wear that kind of tie because it's an off-shade green."

"Listen," she said, "he'll wear anything I buy him—he's dead!"

LAURIE, JR.

A teacher of chemistry was conducting a class. "What can you tell me about nitrates?" he asked one particular student.

"All I know about 'night rates,' " confessed the elected one, "is that they're cheaper than 'day rates.' "    FORD

A woman called up the owner of a restaurant. "Would you mind calling my husband, Barney the waiter, to the phone?"

"Barney, the waiter?" he asked. "Does he work for me?"

"Yes," she informed, "but just at present he's outside picketing the place." HERSHFIELD

The mistress of a home heard a terrible groaning in her kitchen. Alarmed, she dashed in and addressed her new cook. "What's the matter, Nora?" she inquired.

"Oh, oh, glory be!" wailed Nora. "You told me to put the turkey in the oven and turn for three hours. I've been turning for an hour and I'm as dizzy as a goat!"

LAURIE, JR.

Talking about efficiency, Bugs Baer once said: "We ought to put wars in the hands of efficiency experts, because anything an efficiency expert has anything to do with doesn't last very long!" FORD

There's a little uptown delicatessen store. The proprietor was asked how many people it could accommodate. "Six," he said. "Without mink coats, forty!" HERSHFIELD

Two morons met. "Gee, I can't sleep at all," complained one.

"Why don't you count sheep?" suggested the other.

"I can't count sheep," confessed the complaining one. "I'm near-sighted—I have to count elephants." LAURIE, JR.

I'm one bird who isn't henpecked. My wife goes her way, and I go—hers! FORD

Speaking of henpecked guys, a wife once remarked to her husband, "I wish I had known you when you were alive!"

HERSHFIELD

A meat market was terribly crowded. People were shoving and pushing each other all around. Finally, the boss noticed one of the butchers arguing with a woman customer. She left in a huff. "What was the matter?" asked the boss. "Oh, she was complaining about the long wait," he replied, then added, "You can't please that woman. Yesterday she was complaining about the short weight."                    LAURIE, JR.

Christmas is the time of the year when both trees and husbands get trimmed. Sometimes both get lit up, too.    FORD

A hillbilly joined the Army. After giving him instructions how to challenge, they put him on sentry duty. The first day he was on duty, his parents came to visit him. "Hello, Mom! Hello, Pop!" he called, then challenged, "who goes there?"

HERSHFIELD

A lawyer got his client a suspended sentence—they hanged him!                    LAURIE, JR.

The most dangerous part of a car is the nut that holds the steering wheel.                    FORD

Any of your friends can become an enemy, but a relative is one from the start!                    HERSHFIELD

An indignant Scotchman sent a letter to the editor of a newspaper. "If you don't stop writing about Scotchmen being so stingy," he penned, "I'll stop borrowing your paper."

LAURIE, JR.

Talking about pictures, I like to prowl around in Art Galleries. Incidentally, I often wonder whatever happened to Whistler's father?                    FORD

One night, Ivan came home to his wife Sonia with lipstick on his collar. "Where did you get that?" she demanded. "From my maid?"

"No," Ivan replied.

"From the governess?" Sonia snapped.

"No," repeated Ivan, then indignantly added, "Don't you think I have my own friends?"                    HERSHFIELD

A fellow went into a clothing store and tried on a coat. "What's the matter with this coat?" he asked. "The shoulders pinch."

"Put on the pants," suggested the shrewd salesman, "they'll be so tight you'll forget all about the shoulders!"

LAURIE, JR.

During World War II we tried to get Turkey to join the Allies. In the war before, Turkey was on the other side and successfully held the Dardanelles Strait against the Allies. In those days, that situation was like a poker game—there were the Allies with three Kings against the Turks with a Strait!! Who couldn't hold a Strait against three Kings?—especially when the Strait was opened on both ends, too!

FORD

Late one night, a farmer noticed a light in his barn, so he went to see what it was all about. He discovered a farm hand with a lantern. "What's the idea of carrying around a lighted lantern when we can use the oil for the war effort?" he asked.

"I'm going to call on a girl for the first time," the farm hand explained. "I've got to go through the woods and it's dark."

"When I was your age calling on my wife for the first

time," said the farmer, "I went through the woods without a lantern."

"Yeah," reminded the farm hand, "but look what you got!"

HERSHFIELD

A woman gave a party for some soldiers, sailors and marines. The perfect hostess, she even went into the kitchen and made some cookies. Later, she came out with a trayful and offered them to a big, husky marine. "I'm the hostess," she said, "would you like a hot cookie?"

"Sorry, Ma'am," he replied, "I have a date already!"

LAURIE, JR.

Dopey Dilldock brought Screwball Jake a present. "Oh boy! That's just what I needed," said Screwball. "What is it?"

"It's a lemon squeezer," informed Dopey.

"It looks more like a statue of Mussolini," reflected Screwball.

"It is a combination of a statue of Mussolini and a lemon squeezer," explained Dopey. "You push the lemon down on Mussolini's head and the juice comes squirting out of his ears!"

FORD

One night, a moron was strolling along a lonely road. Suddenly, there was a flash of light and a ghost appeared! "What do you most desire?" asked the ghost.

"A hot dog," replied the foolish one. The ghost nodded, then disappeared in a puff of smoke. Twenty years later, the same moron was strolling along the same lonely road. A flash of light and the same ghost appeared! "How do you want your hot dog?" asked the ghost. "With mustard," said the moron.

HERSHFIELD

A fellow with a big red nose went into a beauty shop. "Have you got some makeup that I can use to cover my nose?" he asked. "Goodness, no!" replied the shocked beautician. "I've never seen a nose like that before—do you do a lot of drinking?"

"No," he replied, "I never drink."

"Pardon me for asking, but how in the world did you ever get a big red nose like that?"

"When they were giving out noses," he explained, "I thought they said 'roses' and I said—'give me a big red one'!"

LAURIE, JR.

Two fellows met. "Is it unlucky to postpone a wedding?" asked one.

"Not if you keep on postponing it!" assured the other.

FORD

A guy walked into a restaurant and carefully perused the menu. The waiter said, "What will you have?"

"What have you got," asked the customer, "that'll give me a heartburn immediately instead of at three o'clock in the morning?"                                        HERSHFIELD

Fred Allen's definition of a shroud is: "It's a windbreaker for a ghost."                                        LAURIE, JR.

Bing Crosby and Bob Burns were on a shopping trip to buy feed for Bing's racehorses. They ended up in a coal yard. "What are we here for?" inquired Bob. "Horses don't eat coal."

"I've tried to make them run fast every other way," explained Bing, "and this year I'm going to try steam!"

FORD

A fellow was spinning wild yarns to Clancy about his numerous thrilling adventures—how he flew over the Alps with one wing broken—how he discovered gold in Alaska by accidentally stumbling over a rock—how he fought a submarine singlehanded during a raging storm in the middle of the Atlantic. After he was all through dreaming it up, he left his bewildered listeners. One of them addressed Clancy. "What do you think of that guy's adventures?" he asked.

"He reminds me of the horns on a steer," said Clancy. "A point here—a point there—and an awful lot of bull in between!"                                      HERSHFIELD

Two friends met. "I'm going to Yellowstone Park," informed one, gleefully.

"That's great," enthused the other. "Don't forget to see Old Faithful."

"See it?" exclaimed the new tourist. "I'm taking her with me!"                                      LAURIE, JR.

I was once Commodore of the Happy Hour Yacht Club. H. I. Phillips says a Commodore is a cross between a humidor and a matador. He has to be damp like a humidor, and bull-throwing like a matador.                                      FORD

One afternoon, there was a raid on a Broadway burlesque show and the patrol wagon backed up against the stage door. Maizie, the read-headed stripper, started pushing everyone out of the way and dashed toward the patrol wagon. "Why the big rush?" asked a cop.

"The last time I had to stand!" snapped Maizie.
                                      HERSHFIELD

A goof kept staring at a man in a restauraunt—much to his discomfort. Finally, he said, "What are you staring at?"

"I beg your pardon," exclaimed the goof, "but you remind me of my wife."

"How do I remind you of your wife?" gasped the amazed man.

"On account of your mustache," exclaimed the daffydill.

"But I haven't any mustache," said the man, now completely bewildered.

"I know," said the goof, "but my wife has."

LAURIE, JR.

On a subway train during the rush hour, a sweet young thing was standing alongside of me. "I beg your pardon," I said, "but do you mind if I find a strap for you?"

"I have a strap," she said icily.

"Then please let go of my necktie!" I said.            FORD

Sandy McPherson fell heir to a million dollars, and all his pals in the saloon he frequented heard about it. Worried that his sudden wealth would change him, Finnegan was discussing it when—in dashed McPherson! He waved them all to the bar. "When McPherson drinks—everybody drinks! When McPherson smokes—everybody smokes!" he shouted.

Finnegan gave him a dirty look and added, "When McPherson pays—everybody pays!"            HERSHFIELD

Bloomberg was watching a parade. He was so jammed in the crowd—he fainted! Excitedly, a man started hollering orders. "Give him air! Clear the way! Get him a glass of water!" he shouted. "Hurry up someone—get him a drink!" Bloomberg's eyes fluttered open and he gasped, "Please, make it a malted!"            LAURIE, JR.

Two oafs were talking. "Are you nuts if you talk to yourself?" asked one.

"No, you ain't nuts if you talk to yourself," assured the other, "but you are if you listen!"

FORD

Somebody asked Gracie Fields what she liked best, Tschaikowsky's "Fifth," or Beethoven's "Ninth." Gracie answered, "Montgomery's 'Eighth'!"

HERSHFIELD

A customer went into a barber shop. "What's the idea of your hands being so dirty?" he asked his favorite tonsorial artist.

"Nobody's had a shampoo today," confessed the barber.

LAURIE, JR.

The cleverness of Ilka Chase is well known. Also that she is very fast on repartee. One day, she went to visit a woman. After ringing the doorbell, the maid appeared. "I'm sorry, Miss Chase," she informed, "but the Madam told me to tell you that she is not in."

"Fine," replied Ilka, "please tell the Madam I'm glad I didn't call!"

FORD

One morning, while shaving, a fellow was cursing and swearing so loudly it attracted the attention of his wife who was preparing breakfast in the kitchen. "What's the matter?" called his young spouse.

"My razor—it won't cut!" he shouted.

"Don't be silly, dear!" she declared. "You mean to tell me your beard is tougher than linoleum?"

HERSHFIELD

A very stout woman went to a doctor's office. "I want to reduce," she said determinedly.

"I'll put you on a vegetable diet then," he said, "with salads, lettuce and lots of other leafy things."

"Will that improve my figure?" she asked, anxiously.

"It certainly will," he assured, "if you keep eating nothing but leafy vegetables."

"Did you ever look at the figure of a rhinoceros?" she asked, skeptically.                              LAURIE, JR.

A highly nervous man was being shaved by a gabby barber. "Shall I go over the chin again?" asked the gabby one.

"No," begged the nervous one, "I heard you the first time!"
                                                        FORD

Laurence D'Orsay, the Englishman, was really a great actor, and the only actor I ever knew that looked exactly like a stage Englishman in real life. On his first visit to America, he had occasion to use the phone for an appointment. "Are you there?" he inquired with the broadest accent conceivable.

"What?" asked the operator, thinking she was being kidded.

"I say, are you there?" repeated D'Orsay. Catching on fast, the operator said. "Are you British?"

"If I were any more British," replied D'Orsay, "I couldn't talk at all!"                              HERSHFIELD

I asked a Lieutenant what G. I. coffee was and he said, "Mud that was drafted!"                              LAURIE, JR.

Talking about speed, Lockheed used to turn out a fighter plane in four hours flat! Five minutes later, a pilot was flying it to his appointed destination. Which reminds me of an appropriate story. During the war, a pilot leaped into one of the Lockheed speed burners, and six hours later the company received the following cablegram: "Landed in Australia. Forgot motor. Please send one."

FORD

A fellow put the following ad in the personal column: Cultured gentleman with bottle of catsup, anxious to meet educated woman with can of beans. Object—matrimony.

HERSHFIELD

A wisecracker went into a restaurant. "I want a piece of pie!" he said.

"Do you want to eat it here or take it out?" asked the waiter.

"I'm going to do both, if you don't mind!" cracked the wise guy.

LAURIE, JR.

Joe Laurie, Jr. was watching a parade one afternoon, and a man alongside of him said, "Are you having a good time, little boy?"

"I'm not a little boy," declared Joe. "Somebody stepped on me!"

FORD

A moron was in a health resort. A new patient arrived. "How long have you been here?" the stranger asked. "Five years," informed the moron. "My doctor sent me down here for arthritis and I'm going to stay here until I get it!"

HERSHFIELD

A dumb dora was reading the latest war news. "What part of the body is a fray?" she asked her husband.

"A what?" he replied.

"A fray!" she repeated.

"How do you spell it?" he asked.

"F-R-A-Y, what part of the body is it?"

"I don't know," he confessed, completely puzzled. "How is it used?"

"Well, it says here in the paper: 'The General was shot in the thick of the fray'!" LAURIE, JR.

A man went into a restaurant and ordered vegetable soup. The waitress brought it. After a couple of spoonfuls, he noticed the tablecloth was wet under the plate. He called the waitress. "Hey, look, sister!" he said. "This tablecloth is wet. There must be a crack in the plate."

"No, that wouldn't have anything to do with it," she assured, then niftied, "that's vegetable soup and maybe there's just a leek in it!" FORD

A salesman's car broke down near an Indian reservation. While waiting for it to be fixed, a big buck came over and watched. "What do you do all day?" the salesman asked the early American.

"Hunt and fish!" was the brief reply.

"What do you hunt?" asked the curious salesman.

"Fish!" replied the Indian. HERSHFIELD

A fellow said he liked his radio better than his wife because he gets less interference from his radio. LAURIE, JR.

Two fellows were standing in a garage. One said, "Do you know how to make anti-freeze?"

"Sure," said the other, "hide her woolen nightgown!"

FORD

A swish went into an ice-cream parlor. "I'd like a soda," he lisped.

"Without what flavor?" asked the clerk.

"Without chocolate," was the response.

"You'll have to take it without vanilla," informed the clerk, after looking over his syrups, "we ain't got no chocolate!"

HERSHFIELD

My father always told me that a fellow with nine hundred and seventy-five thousand dollars is just as happy with a million.

LAURIE, JR.

Two kids were bragging about their respective fathers. "My father is a trustee in Penn State!" boasted one.

"That's nothing," sneered the other. "My father is a trusty in State Pen!"

FORD

"I'm going to take you to a show tomorrow night to see Eddie Cantor," said a fellow to his friend.

"I don't care to see Eddie Cantor," informed the friend.

"Did you ever see Eddie Cantor act?" asked the self-appointed host.

"No, and I don't care to," replied his friend.

"What kind of an attitude is that?" inquired the serious one. "You never saw Eddie Cantor act and you don't want to! Just why don't you want to see Eddie Cantor?"

"I saw an imitator of him once," confessed the friend, "and he was terrible!"

HERSHFIELD

One fellow questioned another. "What kind of a lawyer is Suskin?"

"Oh, Suskin," said the other, "he's got an ambulance bell under his coat!"

LAURIE, JR.

A schoolteacher was conducting her class. "What's the opposite of 'misery'?" she asked a pupil.

"Joy!" was the quick reply.

"Correct," she said. "Now what's the opposite of 'sorrow'?"

"Happiness," answered the pupil.

"Correct," she said. "Now what's the opposite of 'woe'?"

"Giddyap!" snapped the pupil.                    FORD

Max died and Sam went to pay his respects. In the house, the widow was standing at the head of the casket. Sam looked down at it and remarked, "Doesn't he look wonderful!"

"Why not?" said the widow with a shrug. "He was in Miami all winter!"                    HERSHFIELD

When Senator Ford was a kid, they used to call him "Asthma" —because he had so many wheezes!                    LAURIE, JR.

Joe Laurie, Jr. used to be a workman. He was a midget window cleaner. He used to go around cleaning people's eyeglasses!                    FORD

Gunboat Sadie was invited to the christening of a baby. It was the first she ever attended. Afterwards she met her friend, Soldier Mary. "I couldn't stand it! I couldn't stand it!" sobbed Sadie.

"Haven't you ever been to a christening before?" asked Mary.

"I couldn't stand it!—I couldn't stand it!" wailed Sadie, ignoring the question.

"What couldn't you stand?" asked the hard-boiled Mary.

"I couldn't stand to see them smash a champagne bottle over a baby's head! I couldn't stand it!"                    HERSHFIELD

The laziest man I ever heard of was too lazy even to brush his teeth, so he'd just put his brush up to his teeth in the morning, and go to see a tennis match!            LAURIE, JR.

Telephoning is like marriage—you don't always get the right party!                                                                    FORD

They say, if you catch a cold and don't attend to it, it will last fourteen days; but if you go to a doctor and take medicine, you can get rid of it in two weeks.            HERSHFIELD

Ginnis and Doyle met. "Did you hear about Clancy?" asked Ginnis.

"What about him?" inquired Doyle.

"He's going down to Florida for his laryngitis," informed Ginnis.

"Oh, he's getting high toned, eh?" sneered Doyle, "getting a new instrument and he hasn't paid for his old piano yet!"

LAURIE, JR.

A little boy said to his father, "Papa, will you please explain the difference between Capital and Labor?"

His father replied, "If you lend money—it's Capital—and when you try and get it back—it's Labor!"            FORD

A fellow was taking a Civil Service examination. "What does the aurora borealis mean?" was the final and deciding question.

"It means," said the completely baffled fellow, "that I don't get the job!"            HERSHFIELD

A barber was shaving himself. "Look out, Tony!" warned his wife, "you'll cut yourself!"

"Why should I be careful?" asked Tony. "I'm no customer!" LAURIE, JR.

Two kids were talking. "Do you know how to tell a lady worm from a gentleman worm?" asked one.

"Oh, sure!" said the other. "You've heard that the worm turns, so if it turns without putting out its hand—it's a lady worm!" FORD

Finnegan rushed to the assistance of Clancy who was shooting it out with a Jap sniper in a wooded corner of Guadalcanal. "Keep away, Finnegan!" commanded Clancy angrily. "Get your own Jap!" HERSHFIELD

A friend of mine from the Coast wrote me that there's a sign outside of a barber shop in San Francisco that says: Japs Shaved Free Of Charge—P.S. Not responsible for accidents. LAURIE, JR.

I know a woman who was so fond of vegetables that she married a fighter with cauliflower ears! FORD

A fellow dashed into the Pennsylvania depot. "When's the next train for Boston?" he asked.

"It's—it's—it's—" stuttered the stranger with great effort, then said, "if—if—if you hadn't asked me, you'd cau—cau—caught it!" HERSHFIELD

A tramp accosted a young girl. "Lady," he said, "I haven't had a bite in days!"—So, she bit him! LAURIE, JR.

There was a woman who called her husband and her dog

by the same name, but you could always tell which one she was speaking to because she always spoke gently to the dog!

FORD

A lawyer learned that a certain fellow had seen an accident, so he went to him and asked him to be a witness.

"Yes, I'll be a witness for you, but," he warned, "I haven't time to go to the rehearsals!" HERSHFIELD

During the first war, two soldiers on furlough met in New York. "You were in Baltimore last week, weren't you?" asked one.

"Yeah," replied the other.

"What hotel did you stop at?" inquired the first soldier.

"At the Yimca," informed the other.

"I never heard of the Yimca," he said. "How do you spell it?"

"Y M C A." LAURIE, JR.

Up in my home town, an oaf by the name of Giddian Ruffner got a job in the general store. His first customer was a man. "What have you got in slacks?" he asked.

"My wife," answered Giddian. FORD

A panhandler stopped a fellow on the street. "Please give me three cents for a cup of coffee," he begged.

"Three cents for a cup of coffee?" exclaimed the fellow. "A cup of coffee is five cents."

"Who buys retail?" asked the panhandler. HERSHFIELD

A woman with henna-colored hair bought a new hat. She decided to have it dyed the same color as her hair, so she took it to Bloomberg's Cleaning and Dyeing Emporium. "Can you dye this henna color?" she asked.

"Sure! Henna color you want!" Bloomberg assured.

LAURIE, JR.

Two quarter-wits met. One said, "Yesterday, I took a girl to tea—I paid for that. Then I took her to dinner, and I paid for that. After, I took her to the theater, and I paid for that. Then I took her to a night club and I paid for that! Do you think I should have kissed her good night?"

"No," declared the other quarter-wit. "I think you did enough for her!"

FORD

Speaking of confusion, there was so much confusion in Washington during the war that the spies couldn't find out a thing!

HERSHFIELD

A colored soldier from Harlem was in charge of some German prisoners. One had a lot of money, but remembering an order forbidding American soldiers to confiscate money of those captured, the Harlemite said to the German, "Hey, Comrade—want to try crap shootin'?"

LAURIE, JR.

An egotist, who thinks he's the answer to every maiden's prayer, strolled into a hotel lobby one afternoon and spotted a very attractive blonde. He sat down beside her and gave her plenty of study. Finally, he said, "What's your name, sister?"

"Grape Fruit!" she snapped.

"Grape Fruit?" he repeated in surprise.

"Yes," she said. "Every time some fresh guy tries to spoon, I hit him in the eye!"

FORD

A fellow had a house right on the Polish-Russian border. No one knew whether the house was in Poland or in Russia. It was decided to appoint a commission to solve the situation and render a verdict. After deciding it was in Poland, the fellow leaped with joy. "Hurrah!" he shouted, "now I don't have to suffer from those terrible Russian winters!"

HERSHFIELD

A woman was reading a newspaper. Suddenly she called her husband. "John, it says here in the paper that after the war everything will be done by just touching a button!"

"That won't help you any," he retorted. "Look at my shirts—you haven't touched a button in years!"

LAURIE, JR.

When you see a husband and wife walking down the street, the one who is two or three steps ahead is the one—that's mad!

FORD

A famous surgeon had the reputation of being able to take the brain out of a person, examine it and put it back. One day some friends brought a patient. The surgeon operated on him and took his brain out. When the surgeon went to the laboratory to examine the brain, he discovered the patient had mysteriously disappeared! Seven years later, he returned to the hospital. "Where have you been for seven years!" asked the amazed surgeon.

The patient replied, "I was a Professor in a Nazi University!"

HERSHFIELD

Every morning I take exercise. First, I take my teeth off the shelf, then crack them one hundred times before I put them in.

LAURIE, JR.

A woman was on a Lexington Avenue street car. "Do you stop at the Waldorf-Astoria Hotel?" she asked the conductor.

"No," he replied, "I have a nice little room over on Second Avenue."                                                FORD

The original nitwit was the boy that poisoned his father and mother, then pleaded for mercy on the grounds he was an orphan!                                                HERSHFIELD

When I was a kid in school I studied geography. I'll never forget the teacher's map!                                LAURIE, JR.

I know an absent-minded fellow who kissed the door and slammed his wife!                                            FORD

A woman in an expensive mink coat entered an exclusive New York restaurant. "I want some caviar," she said to the waiter, "and please see that it's imported, because I can't tell the difference."                                    HERSHFIELD

A farmer was telling how cold it was on his farm one winter. "The ground was so cold," he ejaculated, "that the hens were laying eggs from a standing position!"           LAURIE, JR.

A customer walked into a barber shop. "How do you want your hair cut?" asked the barber. "Off!" replied the customer.                                                    FORD

"How do you spell 'imbecile'?" the teacher asked little Johnny.

"I-M-M-B-U-S-S-U-L," spelled Johnny.

"The dictionary," she corrected, "spells it 'I-M-B-E-C-I-L-E.'"

"You asked me how *I* spell it!" replied Johnny.

                                                HERSHFIELD

Two women were discussing men and their manners. "See that chap over there?" remarked one. "He has manners. Yesterday at lunch, I dropped my purse and he kicked it over with his foot and said, 'Now lady, you won't have to lean over so far to reach it'!" LAURIE, JR.

A fellow was discussing his ailments. "I've got rheumatism in my left leg," he said.

"That's old age," assured his friend.

"You're crazy!" retorted the fellow. "My right leg is as old as my left one and I haven't got any rheumatism in that one!" FORD

During a terrific storm in the middle of the Atlantic, a Captain in our Fleet realized he had a spy on board his ship. "Who can pray?" he asked looking squarely at the spy.

"I can," assured the spy.

"You'd better start," advised the Captain. "We're one life preserver short!" HERSHFIELD

The first telephone gag was when Daniel went into the Den and found the Lion (line) busy! LAURIE, JR.

A teacher addressed a small pupil. "Give me a brief biography of Benjamin Franklin," she said.

"Well," began the little miss, "Benjamin Franklin was born in Boston. He traveled to Philadelphia. He met a lady who smiled at him. He got married and discovered electricity!" FORD

A fellow asked busy Walt Disney if he ever had the desire to exercise, and Walt replied, "Yes, but when I have the desire to exercise, I always lie down on a couch until the desire passes!" HERSHFIELD

Ever since I was born I've been getting growing pains. Really, I'm getting old and it gives me a pain!  LAURIE, JR.

A tramp went to the back door of a farm house. "Have you got any cake?" he asked the lady.

"Cake?" she repeated in surprise. "Isn't bread good enough for you?"

"Ordinarily, yes," confessed the tramp, "but today is my birthday and I want to celebrate!"  FORD

Whenever anyone talks of birthdays, it reminds me of two fellows. One said, "I saw Sam on the street—he looks ninety! How old is he?"

"One hundred!" said the other fellow.  HERSHFIELD

A Scotchman didn't have any Turkish towels in his bathroom so, after taking a bath, he'd throw tacks on the floor, then jump over them until he got dry!  LAURIE, JR.

Two lunkheads were at a dinner party. One said, "Will you please pass me the bonbons?" The other remarked, "Sweets to the sweet—pass me the nuts!"  FORD

I heard about a moron who refused to die unless they put his shoes on. He didn't want to hurt his feet when he kicked the bucket!  HERSHFIELD

I like the story about the two goofs. One's trousers were terribly crushed. The other reprimanded him for being so sloppy. "I can't have my pants pressed," whined the goof.

"Why can't you?" asked the other.

"Because every place I go to have my pants pressed, they

have a sign in the window that says—'Pants Pressed On The Inside'—and I want mine pressed on the outside!"

LAURIE, JR.

Dopey Dilldock got a job as a clerk in a haberdashery. A man entered and asked for a pair of gloves. "What color?" inquired Dopey.

"Coffee color," replied the customer.

"With or without cream?" asked Dopey.     FORD

Smoked salmon is herring with high blood pressure!

HERSHFIELD

A sailor went into a jewelry store and a glamorous-looking salesgirl waited on him. He selected a diamond ring. "How much?" he asked.

"One hundred dollars," informed the glamorous one.

"Would you take anything off for cash?" he inquired.

"Listen, sailor," she cracked, "this is a jewelry store—not a burlesque show!"     LAURIE, JR.

A woman came into a store to purchase a present for her father. "How about a necktie?" suggested the salesman.

"No," she said, "he has a beard."     FORD

Harry Rappaport had owed Ben Mayer one hundred dollars for a long time, so Ben finally became incensed and dictated the following letter to his stenographer: "Harry Rappaport. As my stenographer is a lady, she wouldn't take a certain kind of letter. As I am a gentleman, I wouldn't take a minute to dictate certain kinds of words, but as you're neither a lady or a gentleman, you've got a pretty good idea of what I mean!"     HERSHFIELD

A fellow was arguing with an Irishman. "The Irish never discover anything!" he said.

"What do you mean, they never discover anything?" exclaimed the incensed Irishman. "A fellow named Kelley discovered one of the best States in the United States!"

"What State?" sneered the agitator.

"The State they named after him—Kelley-fornia!" said the Irishman triumphantly.  LAURIE, JR.

A mental delinquent went into a department store to buy a pillowcase. "What size?" asked the saleslady.

"I don't know," he said. "I wear a size seven hat!"

FORD

Two fellows were standing on a street corner. Two women were approaching. "Here comes my wife and my sweetheart!" gasped one.

"I was just going to say the same thing," remarked the other, calmly.  HERSHFIELD

A hobo accosted a General in Guadalcanal. "Can you give me two bits?" he begged.

"I'm General MacArthur—I give no quarter!" was the reply.  LAURIE, JR.

Elmer Smudgegunk went into his boss's office and asked for a raise. "Can you give me two good reasons why you should get a raise?" asked his boss.

"Sure," replied Elmer. "Twins!"  FORD

Two partners decided they needed a hostess in their office so they advertised in the papers for one. After an interview with a big buxom blondine, the partners excused themselves to discuss her in private. "She won't do," protested one, "she's too big in the first place."

"In the second place, too," agreed the other.

HERSHFIELD

A woman went away for a vacation. One day she phoned her husband: "Darling, this is wonderful!" she gushed. "I've been here exactly four weeks and I've lost half my weight! May I stay a little longer?"

"Sure," he said. "Stay four weeks more!"     LAURIE, JR.

Dugan was in the hospital. His pastor came to visit him. "I'm going to pray so you'll forgive Casey for hitting you with a brick," he said.

"It might be better, Your Reverence," suggested Dugan, "if you waited until I get well and then pray for Casey!"

FORD

A fellow called by the Draft Board was examined by his family doctor who happened to be on the board. He passed easily and was put in the Army, which burned him up. He returned to see the doctor. "You're a fine doctor," he blurted. "It's funny you always found something the matter with me when I was paying you five dollars a visit!"     HERSHFIELD

Jake asked Abe, "How long are you in business?"

"I was born in 1890," answered Abe.     LAURIE, JR.

A teacher said to a pupil, "Define an onion."

"An onion," explained the pupil, "builds you up physically and tears you down socially!"     HERSHFIELD

A group of women were playing bridge. "You have beautiful diamonds, Mrs. Blumberg," complimented one.

"Humph—last year's!" said Mrs. Blumberg.

LAURIE, JR.

Two dopes met. "Where are you living now?" asked one.

"With my sister," said the other.

"Where does your sister live?" asked the first.

"With me," informed the other.

FORD

Here's the modern version of "Joe, The Fireman":

> Oh, Fireman, Fireman, save my life!
> As flame and smoke arose . . .
> She's now his wife, he saved her life,
> He brought the Nylon hose!

HERSHFIELD

At the dinner table, a father asked his little son about his conduct in school. "The teacher made me stand with my face to the wall today," confessed the boy.

"You must have done something bad to be punished that way," exclaimed his father.

"She didn't punish me," explained the little boy. "She was trying to fix her garter!"

LAURIE, JR.

Two quarter-wits were arguing. "You're a perfect dope!" exclaimed one, exasperated.

"Don't be kidding," advised the other, "none of us is perfect!"

FORD

That house painter, Hitler, must have been sorry he wasn't color-blind at the end of the war—because the more he saw red, the bluer he got!

HERSHFIELD

No. 111470 was sentenced for first-degree murder. As the day approached, the Warden came to visit him. "I want to make it comfortable for you, so I'll put a sofa in your cell."

"No, don't," protested the numbered one. "I want a Morris chair."

"Sofa," insisted the Warden.

"Morris chair," argued the doomed man. Well, it finally wound up that he got—the chair! LAURIE, JR.

In my home town, the news was circulated that a well-known landlady had run away with her star boarder, but it turned out to be only a roomer! FORD

This is a droll, delightful bit of stupidity I read today in Walter Winchell's column: The imitation of a Hollywood wolf—"Howwwwwwwww old are you?" HERSHFIELD

Two daffydills met on the street corner. "I've got to go to a doctor," groaned one. "I've got a floating kidney!"

"You don't need a doctor!" assured the other.

"No?" asked the first one hopefully. "What will I do with the floating kidney?"

"Put an outboard motor on it!" advised the other.

LAURIE, JR.

Tillie Numbnut got a letter from her boy friend and immediately rushed to a cooking school. "I must learn how to bake right away!" she gasped breathlessly. "Because my boy friend who's in jail wrote me to bake him a hack-saw pie!"

FORD

I like the definition of a radical orator: A fellow who minds his own business at the top of his voice! HERSHFIELD

Every day, Doyle was outside the cemetery gates. "What's the idea of standing outside the cemetery gates?" asked a friend.

"A few years ago," explained Doyle, "I loaned Guiness fifty dollars. He's got to pass through here some day!"

LAURIE, JR.

A man was hailed into the speeder's court. "What's your excuse for driving sixty miles an hour?" asked the Magistrate.

"I couldn't have been driving sixty miles an hour," said the man. "I haven't been out an hour yet!"     FORD

A customer came into a restaurant for breakfast. He called the colored waiter. "A couple of soft-boiled eggs," he said.

"Yassuh!" crooned the waiter.

"Are they fresh eggs?—country eggs?"

"Yassuh!" replied the sepia one.

After he brought the order the customer opened the eggs and let out a squawk: "These eggs are terrible!" he exclaimed. "I thought you said they were from the country?"

"Yassuh, Boss, de old country!"     HERSHFIELD

One afternoon, while relating an experience to a group of fellows, Frank Buck, the big-game hunter, remarked, "Do you know, gentlemen, that if you carry a white stick a tiger won't touch you?"

Whereupon a fellow cracked, "Oh, yeah? How fast must you carry it?"     LAURIE, JR.

Speaking about Frank Buck—when an elephant gets drunk it sees pink Frank Bucks!     FORD

Two morons went to a lecture to hear a scientist. He was explaining how heat expands and cold contracts. One moron nudged the other, "Hear that?" he whispered. "Heat expands and cold contracts!"

The other moron nodded knowingly. "Sure," he said, "that's why days are longer in summer and shorter in winter!"  HERSHFIELD

Two fellows were arguing about books. One argued that the Bible is the greatest book—the other stood pat for the dictionary. "You've got to know how to spell a word before you can even look it up in a dictionary!" he said.

LAURIE, JR.

Sam and Max were in their office. Suddenly Max called, "Sam, catch me! I'm dizzy!"

"What made you dizzy?" asked Sam.

"I was reading a circular letter!" gasped Max.  FORD

I just heard why Solomon had a thousand wives—he figured that when he came home at night at least one wouldn't complain about a headache!  HERSHFIELD

I have an uncle who is very fat. He weighs over three hundred and fifty pounds! To give you a slight idea of how fat he is, one day he stooped down to tie his shoe lace and two women got on his back mistaking him for the bus!

LAURIE, JR.

One day, shortly after the Ockie Bopps had their first baby, Ockie said to his wife, "Don't you think it's about time that the baby called me Daddy?"

"No," replied Mrs. Bopp. "I've decided not to let him know who you are until he gets a little stronger!"  FORD

I've often wondered why fat women always sing "I'd Climb
The Highest Mountain!"                             HERSHFIELD

One time Jimmy Durante went to a circus. Seated next to him
was a little kid who was trying to stuff peanuts up Jimmy's
nose. "Stop that!" protested Jimmy.
    The kid turned to his mother in surprise and said, "Gee,
Mom! The elephant can talk!"                       LAURIE, JR.

A boy said to his Mother, "Mom, you know that vase in the
living room that's been handed down from generation to
generation?"
    "Yes," replied his Mother. "What about it?"
    "This generation dropped it!" he explained.        FORD

I always read the *Times* first—every bit of it—then I buy the
*Mirror* to verify what I read!                    HERSHFIELD.

There's a big sign outside a laundry which says: "Don't kill
your wife—let us do your dirty work!"              LAURIE, JR.

Ditsey Baumwortle and Screwball Jake are two oafs who
think that 'Art' is short for 'Arthur'!                 FORD

Will Rogers had the solution to the congested traffic situation. He proposed that streets could only be used by autos
that were paid for!                                HERSHFIELD

The other day in the subway, I discovered why they have
mirrors in those chewing-gum machines. That's so you can
see how you look when the gum doesn't come out!
                                                   LAURIE, JR.

Nowadays when you take a girl out driving and tell her you're out of gas—she knows you're not fooling!   FORD

A famous conversation between a flirtatious boy and a love-sick girl at a Bronx dance hall.
"Are you dancing?" says he.
"Are you asking?" says she.
"I'm asking," says he.
"I'm dancing," says she.   HERSHFIELD

Mrs. Epstein went into a grocery store. "How much are eggs?" she asked.
"Well," explained the grocer, "we've got first grade, second grade, and—"
"Wait a minute," interrupted Mrs. Epstein, "give me graduated eggs!"   LAURIE, JR.

A jury was being impaneled. The attorney for the defense was challenging prospective jurors. He questioned a little thin man. "Are you married or single?" he asked.
"Married—for ten years," he replied.
"Have you formed or expressed an opinion?" asked the attorney.
"Not for ten years!" confessed the henpecked one.   FORD

Max and Sam had just finished a terrific argument. Finally, they made peace, shook hands and went into a saloon for a drink. Sam lifted his glass in a toast to Max.
"Here's wishing you what you're wishing me!" he toasted.
"Are you commencing again?" questioned Sam, pugnaciously.   HERSHFIELD

A beggar painted his hands with luminous paint so they could be seen in a blackout! LAURIE, JR.

A stingy man was bawling out his wife for buying a fire extinguisher. He said, "What's the idea of spending money for a fire extinguisher when we elected Mayor LaGuardia to put out the fires?" FORD

A girl who worked in an ammunition plant went to the country to spend her vacation. She sent her boy friend a souvenir postal card. On it was written—"Having a wonderful time-and-a-half!" HERSHFIELD

A screwball dashed breathlessly into a hardware store. "Hey, Mister!" he shouted. "Have you got any nails?"
"Yes," was the reply.
"Then scratch my back!" demanded the screwball.
LAURIE, JR.

I know a fellow who was so popular that New Year's Eve he received an invitation from the Astors, the Vanderbilts and—the Draft Board! FORD

They say that in your dreams, you meet a better class of people! HERSHFIELD

A kid entered his house, "Hey, Mom!" he called, "who put that statue under the sink?"
"Ssh!" warned his Mother. "That's a plumber!"
LAURIE, JR.

In my home town, there's a woman who is nuts about a fur coat, so I brought her a bag of nuts! FORD

An irritable old man was looking for his glasses. "Where's my glasses?" he growled.

"On your nose," reminded the maid.

"Be more definite!" he commanded. HERSHFIELD

A woman went into a grocery store. "How much are eggs?" she inquired.

"Eighty cents a dozen," informed the clerk.

"Eighty cents? That's terrible!" she protested.

"That's on account of the defense program, Madam," he said.

"What's defense got to do with eggs?" she asked.

"Hens are making shells!" he explained. LAURIE, JR.

Did you hear of the college graduate who thought he wasn't allowed to be married because he had a bachelor's degree?

FORD

Max and Sam attended a big shindig. "What kind of a party can they give in rationing times like this?" asked Max. "And I'm so hungry I could eat a horse without mustard!"

"We're going to get mustard, too!" assured Sam.

HERSHFIELD

A hillbilly came to the City and saw an ice-cream cone for the first time—so he bought one. He put the ice cream in his hand, then returned and said, "Here's your holder back, Mister!" LAURIE, JR.

A definition of a widower—the only man with an angel for a wife! FORD

After many years' absence, a man returned to his old boarding house and found a cat in the room he used to occupy. "You finally got a cat," he remarked to the landlady.

"Yes," she replied, "one day she wandered in, discovered we had mice and air-conditioning and decided to stay!"

HERSHFIELD

A woman entered a butcher shop and said, "I'd like a dollar's worth of steak."

The butcher replied, "Come back here and I'll let you smell the hook!"

LAURIE, JR.

An owner of a race horse calls him "Lollipop," because the more you lick it the faster it goes!

FORD

A teacher questioned a small pupil. "What is cowhide used for?" she asked.

"To hold the cow together, for one thing!" replied the imaginative one.

HERSHFIELD

The first people who started clubs were the Indians—Indian clubs!

LAURIE, JR.

A man who had trouble with his eyes wrote the following testimonial to his oculist: Dear Doctor. For years, I saw black spots in front of my eyes, then I took your advice and got glasses. Now, I can see the spots much better!

FORD

A wacky drunk went into a theater. Suddenly, he hollered, "Is there a doctor in the house!"

A man got up and announced, "I'm a Doctor!"

"Hy'ah, Doc!" said the drunk. "How do you like the show?"

HERSHFIELD

One night in a Catskill Mountain hotel there was an argument in a room that could be heard all over the place. "What's all the noise about?" asked a guest.

"They're having a battle of wits," informed the proprietor.

"Who's in the room?" asked the guest.

"Shimkowitz, Lefkowitz and Horowitz!"     LAURIE, JR.

A man grabbed the phone and shouted, "Hurry, get me a Doctor! My wife has appendicitis!"

"I'll get you the Chief Operator," cooed the girl at the switchboard.                                      FORD

One cannibal said to another, "Who is that lady I saw you with at the picnic?"

"That was no lady," replied the other, "that was my lunch!"                                      HERSHFIELD

A wise guy said to his butcher, "Give me a porterhorse steak!"                                      LAURIE, JR.

The railroad that takes me up to my home town is going to speed up the service—they're going to put the stations closer together!                                      FORD

It took a goof twenty years to realize that there was no cottage in cottage cheese!                   HERSHFIELD

An egotistical author called on John Golden, the famous producer. "Did you read my play?" he inquired.

"It was so bad," confessed Mr. Golden, "that we had to rewrite it before we threw it into the wastepaper basket!"

                                      LAURIE, JR.

Talk about being crushed and squeezed in a crowded subway train—I know a man who got in one with a copy of *Grapes of Wrath* and when he got off he had a handful of wine!                                        FORD

A fellow always smoked a small stub of a cigar. "I always see you smoking a butt—you certainly get your money's worth, don't you?" remarked a friend.

"That's an Al Smith cigar," informed the fellow.

"What do you mean, an Al Smith cigar?" asked the friend.

"From the sidewalks of New York!" he replied.

                                        HERSHFIELD

An excitable little American from the Bronx visited the race track in Mexico City. He went to a bookmaker and said, "Ten dollars on Shasta Rose!"

"To win?" asked the bookie.

"What, then, to lose?" asked the Bronxman.    LAURIE, JR.

A country visitor questioned a farmer, "How does the land lie around here?"

"It ain't the land that lies," informed the farmer, "it's the real-estate agents!"                          FORD

"Everybody in my neighborhood takes me for a newly arrived refugee," remarked a woman, "because I'm the only woman in my neighborhood that hasn't got a mink coat!"

                                        HERSHFIELD

A grandmother came to visit her grandchild. It was the first time they had ever met. "Who are you, lady?" asked the grandchild.

"I'm your grandmother," she gushed, "on your father's side!"

"You're on the wrong side," informed the youngster.

LAURIE, JR.

The discussion was ancestry. "Did you ever have your family traced?" inquired an Eastern socialite.

"Only my uncle," replied the other. "They traced him as far as San Francisco before they caught him!"     FORD

A husband was complaining to a pal about rationing going too far. "My wife is rationing my kisses," he said. "She only gives me two kisses a week!"

"What are you complaining about?" remarked the pal. "She cut off all your friends completely!"     HERSHFIELD

Two little Brooklyn urchins were day dreaming. "I wish I was a boid," said one. "I'd fly all over the woild!"

"I wish I was an elephant," said the other, "then I could squirt water through me nose!"     LAURIE, JR.

My mother-in-law visits us only twice a year, but she stays six months each time!     FORD

A wolf, anxious to escort a girl home in a taxi, said, "We'll have a nice little talk." She fell for his line. As soon as they entered the taxi he put his arms around her.

"I see you talk with your hands!" she said with meaning.

"Oh, sure," confessed the wolf, "but I'm only whispering now, Toots!"     HERSHFIELD

Two kids were arguing. "Don't say I stole your nickel!" warned one.

"I'm out a nickel and you're eating peanuts!" insinuated the other.                                    LAURIE, JR.

I know a Civil War golfer—he went out in sixty-one and came back in sixty-five!                    FORD

MacPherson and Ginsberg were discussing the necessity of saving money these days. "The other day I walked down Broadway—I didn't take a street car," informed the Scotchman, "and I saved five cents!"

"What kind of a Scotchman are you?" asked Ginsberg. "Why didn't you walk down Fifth Avenue, refuse to take a bus and save ten cents?"                    HERSHFIELD

A little kid passed a candy store the other day and said, "We don't know where Mom is but we've got Pop on ice!"
                    LAURIE, JR.

Fred Allen told me that the phenomenon he would like to see would be statues flying around pigeons!                    FORD

"Did you hear what happened to the girl who wore cotton stockings?" questioned a fellow.

"No, what happened?" asked his friend.

"Nothing!" assured the fellow.                    HERSHFIELD

A woman complained to her husband, "You don't look at me any more—you don't love me!"

"How can I look at you and love you?" asked the frank husband.                    LAURIE, JR.

I know a fellow who is so fastidious that one day he went into a bakeshop but refused to buy some ladyfingers because they weren't manicured!                    FORD

A not too bright cop was taking a desperado to jail. While crossing a street the desperado's hat blew off and he started as if to chase it.

"No you don't, wise guy!" warned the cop. "You stay where you are and I'll get it!"  HERSHFIELD

Mrs. Rappaport went to the Air Mail window in the Post Office to buy a stamp. "I'd like to have a stamp," she said.

"What kind?" asked the clerk.

"What kind?—what a question!" she remarked; then explained, "It should fly!"  LAURIE, JR.

A man went to the office of the Electric Light Company. "Why did you cut off my current?" he asked.

"You didn't pay your bill," informed the clerk. "No currency—no current!"  FORD

Late one afternoon, Sam returned home unexpectedly and found his very homely three-hundred-pound wife being kissed by his pal, Max.

"Listen, Max," protested Sam, "*I* must—but what's *your* reason?"  HERSHFIELD

"Papa, buy me an ice-cream cone," pleaded a little kid.

"Wouldn't you rather wait until you're twenty-one?" inquired his father. "Then I'll buy you an automobile!"  LAURIE, JR.

Two women were talking about a recent burglary. "Was your husband cool when he saw the burglar?" inquired one.

"Was he cool?" echoed the other. "He was so cool, he was shivering!"  FORD

World War II was a question of timing—Big Ben of London against the Watch on the Rhine!          HERSHFIELD

"Honorable Captain," said a Japanese officer, "we cannot take Hill 707 for four reasons!"
  "What's the four reasons?" demanded the Captain.
  "One Irishman and three bricks!" reported the Japansey.
                                                      LAURIE, JR.

At Teheran, Roosevelt, Churchill and Stalin were conferring. "What's cooking?" asked a war correspondent. "Hitler's goose!" chorused the three.                        FORD

An insurance agent went to call on a male client. He rang the doorbell and a woman admitted him. After greeting his client, the agent asked, "Was that your wife who let me in?"
  "Do you think I'd hire a maid as homely as that?" inquired the client.                                    HERSHFIELD

A fellow went into a bird store. "I wanna pet," he said.
  "Why don't you try the balcony of the Paramount?" suggested the salesman.                              LAURIE, JR.

Two fellows were gabbing. "I'm a self-made man," bragged one.
  "That's what comes of hiring cheap labor!" remarked the other.                                                FORD

A chafing dish is a frying pan that got into society!
                                                      HERSHFIELD

"You know I'm a hero?" said a fellow to another. "How come you're a hero?" asked the other.

"You see, it was my gal's birthday," explained the fellow, "and she said 'if you ever brought me a gift I'd drop dead'! So, I didn't buy her any and saved her life!" LAURIE, JR.

There's a night club in Hollywood where they have a midget fan dancer for the guests who are under the table! FORD

At a church festival, punch was served. It was quite potent. An usher, whose duty was to see that everyone was properly placed, had a few drinks too many. Suddenly, he noticed a woman in the wrong seat.

"Pardon me, Madam," he said with great dignity, "but this pie is occupued!" HERSHFIELD

"I don't like these shoes!" complained a female customer to a salesman. "Because after a couple of years—they spread."

"Didn't you?" he asked. LAURIE, JR.

Ditsey Baumwortle had two bosses, one he worked for and the other he was married to! FORD

A fellow went to eat in a Hungarian restaurant for the first time and didn't know what to order. "The goulash is wonderful!" suggested the boss. So, the fellow ordered it. After he was through eating it—he belched! He looked at the boss, suspiciously.

"What do you expect?" asked the boss. "Chimes?"

HERSHFIELD

I remember years ago when a horse would see an automobile and get frightened. Now, the only time a horse gets frightened is when he sees another horse! LAURIE, JR.

A Papa Kangaroo said to a Mama Kangaroo, "Where's our kiddie?" She looked in her pouch, "Ye Gods!" she yowled. "My pocket's been picked!"                                      FORD

In a circus, a recently engaged colored helper was instructed to feed a lion. "Not me," protested the sepia one.

"What are you afraid of?" asked the boss. "Didn't you ever hear of Daniel in the Lion's Den?"

"Listen, man," said the helper, "de lion's den and de lion's now are altogether different!"                                      HERSHFIELD

A kid was reading the paper. "Hey, Poppa!" he called. "It says in the paper that the Gulf Stream is changing its course."

"What do I care?" replied his father. "I don't play golf!"
                                      LAURIE, JR.

A man returned home one night in a rage. "The world's full of crooks these days!" he raved to his wife. "Just today a guy tried to clip me with a phoney quarter and if that bartender around the corner wasn't so near-sighted—I never would have gotten rid of it!"                                      FORD

A little girl who had never seen a peacock before visited her grandmother who had one in the barnyard of her country home. It was strutting around with its tail fanned. The little girl ran into the house and called, "Grandma! Grandma! Come out quick! One of your chickens is in full bloom!"
                                      HERSHFIELD

A fellow said he had a great job in Times Square—keeping the Sailors away from the Waves!                                      LAURIE, JR.

Over at our house, we've got those meatless Tuesdays out-figured. At lunch we have calves' brains and for dinner we have oxtail. That's one way to make both ends meat! FORD

I know a farmer who packed up and moved to the city when he heard the country was at war! HERSHFIELD

Two friendly taxi drivers stopped at an intersection. "How's your old jalopy?" inquired one.
"Fine!" said the other. "How's your wife?"

LAURIE, JR.

I know a wolf who is a big dame hunter! FORD

An office boy went to his boss and said, "Say, Boss, can I go to the ball game this afternoon? My grandmother's playing third base!" HERSHFIELD

Two soldiers were driving a jeep. One remarked, "We must be getting near camp—we're knocking down fewer civilians!"

LAURIE, JR.

Ditsey Baumwortle returned as hot as a ball of fire from the butcher shop. "What are you so angry about?" asked his wife.
"When I asked the butcher for ten cents' worth of dog meat," sizzled Ditsey, "the butcher said, 'shall I wrap it or will you eat it here'?" FORD

In India, there's over forty-three million untouchables. Of course, there's millions of untouchables in this country, too—if you every try to make a touch! HERSHFIELD

Two colored men got into an argument. "Doan start pickin' on me!" warned one. "Ah was decorated in de last war fo' bravery!"

The other said, "Get ready to be decorated again!"

LAURIE, JR.

A doctor remarked to Screwball Jake, "You know, Screwball, exercise kills germs."

"How do you get the germs to exercise?" asked Screwball.

FORD

I know a philosopher who likes to travel in his own car. When he's driving he says he runs across so many interesting people!

HERSHFIELD

A Scotch woman owned a small apartment building. Her husband got sick and ran a high fever. When it got up to one hundred and three she put him in the cellar to heat up the building!

LAURIE, JR.

Two fellows met. One said, "Where are you working?"

The other replied, "I'm not working at all. I was working in a defense plant but they fired me."

"They can't fire you if you work in a defense plant," informed the other. "Don't you know you're frozen there?"

"That's what I told the foreman," explained the absentee, "but he caught me asleep, so he defrosted me!"

FORD

A woman went into a department store to purchase a new spring hat. "I'd like to try on that hat over there," she said to the saleslady.

"That's not a hat," declared the saleslady, "that's a tomato surprise!"

HERSHFIELD

Mike was brought into court for being plastered. "Where did you get the liquor?" demanded the Judge.

"A Scotchman gave it to me," whimpered Mike.

"Ten dollars for perjury!" thundered his Honor.

LAURIE, JR.

A cynic once said that some women are like poorly made photographs—underdeveloped and overexposed! FORD

A live-wire salesman approached the manager of a factory. "I'd like your approval to sell your workingmen a course that would spark and put fire into their work."

"Get out of here!" ordered the manager. "This is a dynamite factory!" HERSHFIELD

A guest in a hotel rushed down to the night clerk. "I just got a hat pin stuck in my eye!" he screamed.

"Through an argument?" inquired the clerk.

"No, through a keyhole!" howled the guest. LAURIE, JR.

A Northerner asked a Southerner, "Is there any other cure for snake bites besides whiskey?"

"Who cares whether there is or not!" drawled the Southerner. FORD

A girl behind the counter of a department store noticed a man waiting. "Could I interest you in a tropical bathing suit?" she asked. "You sure could, kid," he confessed, "but my wife's around here some place!" HERSHFIELD

That's like the guy who died and willed his floating kidney to the Aquarium! LAURIE, JR.

# 3

## CAN YOU TOP THESE?

*Top-notch Stories and Jokes*

SEE IF YOU CAN GUESS WHAT THESE JOKES
REGISTERED ON THE STUDIO LAUGH METER

Note: Turn to back of book for Laugh Meter
scores.

**1**

In my book *Among The Delphiniums With Ditsey Baumwortle* there's a passage in which Ditsey is talking to a fellow. The conversation goes something like this:

"Hello! Ditsey, I ain't seen you around of late, lately. Where have you been?"

"Oh, I went on a trip," explains Ditsey. "I found out the best way to get someplace is to travel to it."

"So I've heard," says Ditsey's friend.

"Me and Phoebe went to Dithington by the Dumps, at Sussex."

"Oh, you went by boat, eh?"

"Yeah."

"Were you seasick?"

"Well, I wasn't but Phoebe was. She was awful seasick. Her whole face was green—a very dark shade of green. In fact, it was so green that one time she opened her mouth to yawn and a fellow mailed a letter in it."          FORD

**2**

One night, a couple were making love on a park bench. They were hugging away for dear life when a cop came by, stopped, and put his flashlight on them.

"You've got a lot of nerve making love in the park!" he said angrily. "You know it's against the law. Come on to the Police Station!"

In court the Judge asked what the charges were and the cop related the scene.

"You both know it's against the law," declared the Judge. "Why did you make love in the park?"

"Well, your Honor," explained the man, "this woman is my wife!"

"That saves you," said the Judge with a grin. "Case dismissed!"

As the couple were leaving, the cop called the man aside to apologize.

"I'm sorry, old man," he said. "I didn't know it was your wife."

"I didn't either," confessed the man with a grin, "until you put that flashlight on us!"                                      HERSHFIELD

## 3

At a cloak and suit convention, this story always "boffs" 'em.

Mrs. Bloomberg met Mrs. Rappaport and Mrs. Epstein on the street and invited them to come up to see her new home and antiques.

"I've got some wonderful 'an-ti-kies' you'd enjoy," she said.

Out of curiosity they visited her.

"She's got wonderful 'an-ti-kies,'" admitted Mrs. Rappaport, "and a very, very wonderful place."

"Look," said Mrs. Epstein. "I wonder where she got that huge chest?"

"I don't know," replied Mrs. Rappaport. "But they say her mother was built the same way!"                                      LAURIE, JR.

## 4

A teacher was explaining hybrids to her class.

"For example," explained the teacher, "if you cross a horse

and a donkey, you get a mule. Now what would happen if you cross a mule with a cow?"

"You'd get milk with a kick in it," shouted a student.

FORD

## 5

Before flying back to England the famous war correspondent, Quentin Reynolds, told this story at a Service Men's night in the Lambs Club.

Sergeant Clancy was known as the grouchiest guy in the Army. The General came for inspection and Clancy started putting his squad through the customary paces, shouting commands in the following manner:

"Shoulder Arms!—the same to you!—Forward March!—the same to you!—Halt!—the same to you!"

The General stopped Clancy.

"Just a minute, Sergeant," he said. "What's going on here? Every time you give an order you add 'the same to you.' What's that all about?"

"Listen, General," Clancy explained. "I'm no dope. Every time I give them an order I know what they're saying to me under their breath!"

HERSHFIELD

## 6

I heard Judge Jonah Goldstein tell this story to the Grand Street boys at one of their get-togethers.

A man was worried about the future of his little son and confided to a friend that he couldn't figure out what career or profession to choose for him. One day he decided to try an experiment.

"I'm going to put him in a room, all alone," he said, "with

only a Bible, an apple, and a silver dollar. If the boy reads the Bible, I'll make him a minister. If he eats the apple, I'll make him a farmer. If he fools around with the dollar, I'll make him a banker."

"Great idea," said his friend.

So the boy was put in the room with the Bible, apple, and silver dollar.

Half an hour later, the anxious father went into the room. His little son was seated on the Bible, eating the apple, with the silver dollar in his pocket.

"What are you going to make of him now?" asked the friend.

"A politician!" replied the father.                    LAURIE, JR.

## 7

Last summer some people rented a place by the beach near our bungalow. One day their little boy rapped on our door.

"What can I do for you, son?" I asked.

"Can I see the skillet that died?" he said.

"The skillet that died?" I repeated, puzzled.

"Yes," answered the boy. "Mama said you have a dead pan!"

FORD

## 8

A fellow married a gorgeous blonde. After three weeks he had to leave on an extended business trip. At the depot he became conscience-stricken at leaving his new bride alone, so he canceled his trip and returned home. Both were very happy. The phone rang. He answered it.

"I'm not in the Navy," he said. "How would I know?"

He hung up and returned to the side of his bride. A few

minutes later the phone rang again. Once more he answered it.

"I'm not in the Navy," he repeated. "How would I know?"

Again he hung up. Curiosity got the better of his bride.

"Who is it, dear?" she inquired.

"Oh, I don't know," he replied. "It's some guy calling and asking if the coast is clear!"                HERSHFIELD

## 9

Tom met Bill on the street and stopped to converse.

"How is it, Bill," asked Tom, "you've always been so nice and happy and since you got married you're so grouchy?"

"Well, I'll tell you," stated Bill. "When I kept company with my wife she kept talking about her buried treasure, so I proposed marriage and she accepted."

"What has that got to do with it?" asked Tom curiously.

"I found out," explained Bill, "that her buried treasure was her first husband."                LAURIE, JR.

## 10

Mr. and Mrs. Snapgirdle got into an argument over furniture.

"Why do you insist upon referring to the folding bed as 'he'?" snapped Mrs. Snapgirdle.

"Because," drawled Mr. Snapgirdle, "you can shut it up once in a while!"                FORD

## 11

Sam always loved to make his friend Max envious, so after refurnishing his home, he invited him over. Sam didn't over-look anything, especially the price of every article, stressing the point that everything was very "expensive." Poor little Max returned home in a very depressed mood. Then someone tipped him off that Sam had bought all the new furniture on the instalment plan. Elated, Max couldn't wait until he got him on the phone.

"Bluffer, you!" he said with contempt. "I found out you bought your furniture on instalments!"

"Sure," admitted Sam. "It's more expensive that way."

HERSHFIELD

## 12

A farmer returned home from New York, which was his first visit to a big city, and met an old friend.

"Did you have a good time, Zeke?" the friend asked.

"Oh, boy, did I!" he enthused. "I walked down Fifth Avenue and all the girls in the store windows flirted with me!"

"Those weren't girls, Zeke," informed his friend. "Those were dummies."

"They weren't so dumb," said Zeke. "They all had mink coats on!"

LAURIE, JR.

## 13

Elmer Smudgegump got a job on a farm. Before he started to work the farmer gave him instructions.

"Elmer," he advised, "you get up at three o'clock in the morning and harvest the oats."

"Three o'clock?" echoed the surprised Elmer. "What are they—wild oats?"

"No," drawled the farmer, "they ain't wild oats."

"Well," asked Elmer, "if they ain't wild oats, what's the idea of sneaking up on them in the dark?"

FORD

**14**

Mr. Clancy was complaining to a neighbor because he couldn't sleep.

"I've got one son who's the bane of my life," explained Clancy. "He's a bum. He worries me so much I can't sleep. It's wearing me down. I haven't had a good night's sleep in months."

"Have you tried counting sheep?" asked his sympathetic neighbor.

"No," answered Clancy. "Is that a good idea?"

"It might be a great help in getting sleepy," advised his neighbor.

Clancy tried it that night. The next morning he looked worse—worn and bedraggled. He met his neighbor again.

"Did you count sheep?" he asked.

"I counted beautifully," Clancy said. "I counted up to ten thousand sheep and was just dozing off, when along came a black sheep. I got to thinking of that bum again and I couldn't sleep the rest of the night!"                HERSHFIELD

**15**

A company of soldiers were out on target practice. Among those present was Private Rappaport. The Lieutenant approached him.

"Rappaport," he said, "what target are you shooting at?"

"Number Four," replied Rappaport.

"How many times have you shot at it?" asked the Lieutenant.

"Ten," confessed Rappaport.

"Do you know you've been hitting the Number Five

target?" informed his superior. "You've hit Number Five exactly ten times!"

"But I was aiming at Number Four."

"But you hit Number Five!"

"Let's call the whole thing off, will you, Lieutenant?" suggested Rappaport. "In fact, you'd better discharge me."

"What do you mean?"

"It ain't no good," confided Rappaport. "Anything is liable to happen with me in the war. I'm liable to be shooting at a Private and hit a General!" LAURIE, JR.

## 16

When Ditsey Baumwortle took his first kid to be christened he carried a bottle of champagne along because he thought they christened kids the way they do ships. Ditsey called the preacher aside.

"I want to have this little son of mine called Maple Syrup Q. Baumwortle, because he's the sweetest little fellow in our family tree."

"But why the middle initial?" asked the preacher. "What does the 'Q' stand for?"

"Oh, the missus added that," Ditsey explained, "because the first time she saw the little fellow she said, 'Hey, Ditsey, let's call it quits'!" FORD

## 17

A shipwrecked sailor met a hermit on an island.

"Are you all alone on this island?" asked the sailor.

"Yeah," answered the hermit.

"What do you do for entertainment?" inquired the sailor.

"I tell jokes to myself."

"Well, that's fine."

"No, it ain't," confessed the hermit. "I keep butting in all the time saying, 'I heard that one before'!"  HERSHFIELD

## 18

When I was a guest at the Press Club in Washington, Henry Kaiser told this story.

A crowd was watching a ship being christened at the shipyards. A woman took a bottle of champagne, hit the ship, and it slid down gracefully into the water. A woman spectator turned to her husband.

"How beautifully it slides down!" she sighed.

"If you were hit with a champagne bottle over the nut you'd slide down beautifully, too!" he assured.  LAURIE, JR.

## 19

Mr. and Mrs. Ditsey Baumwortle had one of those knockdown drag-out arguments. Finally peace reigned because Ditsey lost, and knew it. Phoebe won, and also knew it. Disconsolately, Ditsey stood by the living room window and gazed out. Something attracted his attention.

"Phoebe," he called. "Come here. I want you to look at something."

She joined him at the window.

"Look at those two horses," he said, "pulling that load of coal over that hill. Why can't we pull together like a couple of horses over the hill of life?"

"The reason we can't pull over the hill like a couple of horses," explained Phoebe, "is because one of us is a jackass!"

FORD

**20**

Sammy went to sleep and had a dream. A goofy little fairy appeared.

"You can have three wishes," said the fairy. "I'll make you a present of anything you want."

"How about a reservation to Miami?" asked Sammy.

"Look on your bureau and you'll find it!"

He did and it was there.

"I would like to get two tickets to see the show *Oklahoma*," was Sammy's second wish.

"They're on the bureau!"

Sure enough, they were!

"I would like to kill Hitler," was Sammy's third and last wish.

Just then the phone rang, awakening him.

"I hate to disturb your dream," said a stern voice, "but you just made a wish that you would like to kill Hitler."

"Yes," confessed Sammy. "That's right."

"Great," said the voice. "This is the Draft Board. You're in 1A!" HERSHFIELD

**21**

Two soldiers up in Alaska were talking about their Christmas presents.

"What did you get from your mother?" asked one.

"I got three nightgowns sewed together," the other replied.

"Three nightgowns sewed together—what's the idea of that?"

"My mother heard the nights are much longer up here!" LAURIE, JR.

**22**

To sneak her Pomeranian dog on the Fourteenth Street bus, Mrs. Printwhistle carried it curled around her hands to make it look like a muff. She sat right in the back of the driver. At Thirty-fourth Street she addressed him.

"Is this Seventy-second Street?" she asked.

"No, Ma'am," he replied.

At Forty-second Street Mrs. Printwhistle addressed him again.

"Is this Seventy-Second Street?"

"No."

Her questions continued to Fifty-ninth Street.

"Look, lady," said the exasperated driver, "when we get to Seventy-second Street, I'll tell you."

"I wish you would," she said. "It's very important."

Later he turned and addressed her.

"Lady! This is Seventy-second Street!"

"Thank you," she gushed graciously, then lifted her little Pomeranian to the window. "See, Gumdrop! That's where Mama used to live!"                              FORD

**23**

A son-in-law was so annoyed at his mother-in-law that he threw her out of a fourth-floor window. In court, the Judge denounced the guilty one.

"Do you mean to say," queried the Judge, "that just because you were annoyed by your mother-in-law you threw her out of a fourth-floor window? Have you any idea how dangerous that was in case somebody was passing by at the time?"

                              HERSHFIELD

**24**

A little old lady was traveling in the upper berth of a train. As it was speeding through the night she awoke the man in the lower.

"A glass of water, please," she gasped. "I can't get the porter."

"Surely," he replied, and got up, donned a robe and brought her a glass of water.

She thanked him, drank it, then retired again. Fifteen minutes later she again awakened the man in the lower with the same request. Courteously, he again brought her a glass of water which she quickly gulped down. After being awakened the fifth time the man became curious.

"Pardon me, Madam," he said, handing her the glass of water, "are you ill?"

"No," she assured him, "but am I thirsty!"     LAURIE, JR.


**25**

Fanny Frittlecroft and Tillie Numbnut were talking about their respective boy friends.

"Your fellow is the stingiest human I ever knew," sneered the Frittlecroft dame. "He never takes you out or gives you any presents!"

"That just goes to show how little you know," snapped Tillie in defense. "He gave me a bottle of cologne for Christmas!"

"What kind?" asked Fanny.

"I don't know," admitted the Numbnut doll, "but every time I pass the swamps, skunks jump up and holler, 'Yoo Hoo!'"     FORD

**26**

A ship carrying an all-English passenger list was on a cruise to the Bahamas. As it neared the shore, everybody on deck went to the rail and began throwing pennies into the water to see the native boys dive for them. The only American on board, a chap from New York, watched for a few minutes, then took out a bright silver dollar from his pocket. He was about to toss it overboard into the water when an Englishman grabbed his arm.

"Stop!" he warned, "or you'll have the Duke of Windsor diving for it!"                    HERSHFIELD

**27**

Dave Sarnoff told me this story at cocktail time in the New York Athletic Club.

A man took his young son for his first visit to Radio City. About to get into the elevator, the little one said:

"Hey, Papa! Let me tell you something."

His father bent down and the kid whispered something in his ear.

"No, no—come on!" answered his father, annoyed.

He led the boy by the hand into the waiting elevator.

"Forty-fifth floor!" he said as the elevator started up.

"Hey, Papa, listen!" the kid began.

"No, I tell you. No!" interrupted his father, knowing the request was repetitious.

As they were whisked up, the kid made several vain pleas to his now exasperated pater.

"Why not?" questioned the boy sadly.

"I don't care how Superman goes up. We're going up this way."                    LAURIE, JR.

## 28

At a doctors' banquet this story got a good laugh:

Two young medical students were taking a test in a hospital of a patient who was perspiring profusely. He was completely covered with a sheet that reached up to his neck. The students stood on either side of the bed. To take the patient's temperature, they had to reach under the sheet. By mistake, they got hold of each other's wrists. They waited a few seconds, each studying his watch. Finally one of them said:

"There's nothing serious about it. In fact, there's nothing the matter with him at all."

"No," said the other young medic, "he's just drunk!"

FORD

## 29

On a certain holiday in which special prayers are said, a House of Worship sold tickets. Strict instructions were given that no one was to be permitted to enter the sacred portals without one. In fact, a man was stationed at the door to see that this order was carried out. A man approached and tried to enter.

"I'm very sorry," he explained. "I haven't got a ticket, but my brother is inside and I would like to talk to him."

"Sorry," the doorman advised, "but you have to have a ticket."

"But my brother is inside," insisted the man, "and it's very important that I talk to him."

"All right," said the doorman, weakening. "Go inside and talk to your brother. But," he warned, "don't let me catch you praying!"

HERSHFIELD

**30**

The laziest man I ever heard of was called Uncle Lem. He was a hermit and lived on the top of a mountain in a cave that had a door on it. One hot summer day, his nephew decided to visit him. He opened the door, and there was Uncle Lem seated in a rocking chair smoking a pipe. Although his nephew greeted him warmly and affectionately, Uncle Lem never answered him. He never spoke one word. After a short while, the nephew left. That winter, there was a terrific snowstorm. The dutiful nephew, wondering how Uncle Lem was faring, decided to pay him another visit. So, after traveling for hours through a blinding snowstorm, he arrived at his destination. Uncle Lem was still seated in the rocking chair—with snow up to his neck!

"What's the big idea, Uncle Lem?" he asked.

"The last time you left me," said Uncle Lem, "you forgot to shut the door!"                              LAURIE, JR.

**31**

Traveling to the country on one of those slow Sunday trains, Mrs. Dopey Dilldock handed the conductor a full ticket for herself and a half-fare ticket for her son, Dopey, Jr. who was seated across from her.

"What's this half-fare ticket for?" queried the conductor.

"For my boy, little Dopey, over there," she answered.

"He's not a boy," said the conductor after giving him a quick once-over, "he's a man!"

"He might be a man now," admitted Mrs. Dilldock sarcastically, "but he certainly was a boy when this train started!"                                        FORD

**32**

Little Pinkus was on the witness stand. One of those tough lawyers was giving him a rough questioning and every time Pinkus answered, the lawyer would sneer at him.

"What do you do for a living?" snapped the lawyer.

"I'm a calciminer," answered Pinkus, "and not a very good one at that."

"Oh, a calciminer, eh?" sneered the lawyer. "What do you think your status is in society?"

"Well," admitted Pinkus, "I couldn't get in the 'Four Hundred,' that I know, but I still feel that I'm doing better than my father did."

"What was your father?" snapped the attorney.

"A shyster lawyer!" answered Pinkus.          HERSHFIELD

**33**

Mrs. Bloomberg met Mrs. Rappaport in the market.

"I hear you've got another baby," said Mrs. Bloomberg.

"Yes," enthused Mrs. Rappaport, "and it's a darling."

"What's this one, the fourth or fifth?"

"The fifth one."

"What are you calling the new baby?"

"It's a little girl, so I call her Ming Toy."

"Why Ming Toy? That's no name for a baby."

"Well," explained Mrs. Rappaport, "I was reading a big book. In the book it said—'every fifth child that is born is a Chinaman.' Who am I to argue?"          LAURIE, JR.

**34**

Two kid brothers were on their back porch. The elder

was eating a piece of cake. The other one was crying. Their mother came out to see what it was all about.

"What's he crying for?" she asked the elder one.

"Because I won't give him any cake," he replied.

"Is his cake all gone?" she asked.

"Yes," he answered, "and he cried when I was eating that, too."                                                        FORD

## 35

At the Breakfast Club in Los Angeles, Donald Douglas, President of Douglas Aircraft, told this story.

Everyone knows how difficult it is to get a ticket to see the World Series. A fellow who had never seen a baseball game before, managed to get one. After the game, when he returned home, a friend asked him all about it.

"The usher started to take me up to my seat," he explained. "He took me up five flights and then he said to me, 'from now on, you go by yourself because my nose bleeds.' So, I started to walk by myself. I walked and walked. Finally, I was so tired, I sat down. I said to a fellow, 'what's the score'? 'I don't know,' he said, 'I'm flying the Mail Plane to Chicago.'"

                                                        HERSHFIELD

## 36

Sam came home very late one night and his worried wife was anxiously waiting for him.

"Why are you so late for coming home?" she asked.

"Yoi," moaned Sam, "what happened to me shouldn't happen to a dog!"

"What happened?" she asked, expecting the worst.

"What happened?" he repeated, then explained, "I was in a restaurant, eating, and some college boys came in. They started to get into an argument about football. The next thing, they're hollering and yelling. One fellow said to me, 'Ain't I right, brother'? So, I said, 'Please keep me out of it, I don't like to argue.' I kept eating. Well, the argument gets worse and worse and louder and louder. Then they start fighting and punching each other. One fellow turned and said to me, 'Ain't I right, brother'? I said, 'Please keep me out of it, I don't like fights or arguments. Well, the fight gets worse. Terrible! They were hitting each other with ketchup bottles!"

"What did you do?" gasped his terror-stricken spouse.

"There was a phone booth in the corner," explained Sam, "and I ran there and locked myself in to get away from it. And to get still further away I called up long distance!"

LAURIE, JR.

## 37

I was in the Dodger dressing room between games of a double header, and Leo Durocher told me this one.

One year, the Brooklyn Club was on a Spring training trip down South. A rookie outfielder from a wide spot in some midwestern road reported for training. He had a badger haircut with nothing underneath. He was good and dumb but could powder that apple. When he hit a ball it would sail right out of the County, and that was before they had a rabbit in every baseball, too. One day, the Brooklyn Club was scheduled to play an exhibition game in one of those little Southern parks where the score-board consists of two rows of nails on which are hung square pieces of tin with white numbers painted on them. The rookie was put in the outfield. In the second inning, he came to bat, got hold of a fast one and knocked it right out of the County—for a home run! Going into the eighth inning, the score was one to nothing—the rookie's homer. To play for defense, the manager decided to replace the rookie with one of his regular outfielders. As soon as the rookie heard he was to be taken out of the game, he strode over to the score-board, unhooked the piece of tin with the number "one" on it, and put it under his arm.

"If you ain't going to let me play," he drawled, "you ain't going to count my run!"          FORD

## 38

Salesmen have a hard time getting hotel accommodations with the situation as it is these days and especially in Washington. Well, a salesman had to go to Washington, and everyone who has been there knows how they crowd them in the beds. After waiting in line for hours, the clerk finally told him he'd have to sleep with another fellow.

"All right," said the tired salesman. "Only one guy?"

"Yes," assured the clerk.

So, the salesman went to the room and in no time was in the land of dreams. Another salesman, with half a bun on, staggered up to the clerk. He, too, wanted a room.

"I've got a room but there's one gentleman in it already," said the clerk.

"Only one?" asked the inebriated one.

"Yes," assured the clerk.

He registered, got into the room, lay in bed and stretched out, not realizing that there were two other fellows in bed with him. Suddenly, he looked up and saw—six feet! The fellow next to him woke up.

"I see six feet," said the drunken one.

"Don't disturb anybody," advised the man he had awakened. "Go to sleep. There's only four feet, anyway—yours and mine."

"I see six feet," insisted the drunk.

"You don't. Look for yourself!"

The drunk staggered out of bed, went to the foot of it and started to count.

"One, two, three, four," he counted, slowly but audibly. "I guess you're right—four feet!" HERSHFIELD

## 39

Moe and Sam were partners and had a little store in the middle of a side street.

"Sam," said Moe, "I think we'd better quit the store. Business is terrible. We haven't done any business in a whole month. I think we'd better close up and look for a job."

"I can't understand it," moaned Moe. "We're not doing any business at all, and here in the paper, Roosevelt says that business is wonderful!"

"Well," mused Sam, "maybe he's got a better location!" LAURIE, JR.

## 40

A little boy went into a country drugstore one afternoon.

"I want five cents' worth of asafetida," he said.

The druggist got a ladder, climbed up to the top shelf, got the asafetida, brought it down, wrapped it up and gave it to him.

"Charge it," instructed the kid.

"What's your name?" asked the druggist.

"Honeyfunkle."

"Here," said the disgusted druggist handing him the small

package, "I'll be darned if I'm going to write 'Honeyfunkle' and 'asafetida' for a nickel!"                              FORD

## 41

There's an old saying that "any friend can become an enemy, but a relative is one from the start"—which inspires this story of Mr. and Mrs. Clancy.

"You know, Clancy," said Mrs. Clancy to her husband, "there's something to that old saying that 'blood is thicker than water,' and relatives are always punching each other on the nose to prove it. So, I want to tell you something. You're always fighting with my relatives. You're never quiet for a moment. You're always starting something. Now, we're going to a picnic tomorrow and I want you to be friendly. You're not going to fight or say anything about my relatives, understand?"

"Yes, my dear," promised Clancy. "Only if they provoke me."

The next day at the picnic everything was fine. Clancy was on his best behavior, saying nothing, but glaring around at everybody. Food was placed on a tablecloth which was spread under a tree. The minute the food appeared, everybody started rushing for it—including Clancy, who got there first. He began eating at a furious pace.

"Clancy!" called his embarrassed wife. "Look at that ant in your pie!"

"Look at your uncle in the potato salad!" he replied, pugnaciously.                              HERSHFIELD

## 42

Bloomberg met Epstein on the street and stopped him.

"Epstein," he said, "are you a friend of Einstein's?"

"Are we friends?" answered Epstein. "Fifteen years we're friends. There's nothing I wouldn't do for Einstein and there's nothing he wouldn't do for me. In fact, for years and years, we've gone through life together, doing absolutely nothing for each other."                                                LAURIE, JR.

## 43

Before Ditsey Baumwortle and Ockie Bopp were married, they roomed together. They were about the same size and build. Each possessed just one suit of clothes. One night, Ditsey had a date, so he pressed his pants. In the process, he burned a hole in the seat. Stymied, he didn't know what to do, so he appealed to Ockie.

"Hey, Ockie," he said. "I've got a date with a girl. Will you lend me your pants?"

"Sorry, Ditsey," said Ockie. "I can't. I'm going out myself tonight."

"Look!" warned Ditsey, "if you don't lend me your pants, you're going to lose my friendship!"

"Listen," replied Ockie, "I can go lots of places without your friendship, but I can't go any place without my pants!"
                                                        · FORD

## 44

A fellow in uniform, recently inducted, went to see a doctor.

"Doctor," he said, "I just got in the Army and look at the uniform they gave me. The trousers are exactly the right length. The sleeves are exactly the right length. The hat fits me perfectly and the shoes are the correct size!"

"What about it?" asked the doctor, curiously.

"My problem is, doctor—am I deformed?"   HERSHFIELD

## 45

One day Bloomberg was shaving and cut his throat. He fainted dead away, so he was rushed to the hospital, where he regained consciousness.

"What's happened?" groaned Bloomberg weakly, unable to remember.

"You accidentally cut your throat," the nurse informed, "so they put you in the hospital here."

"I'm hungry," moaned Bloomberg. "What am I paying here?"

"Eight dollars a day for the room and eight dollars a day for a nurse," she replied.

"Eight dollars a day without food?" he asked.

"You can't eat," she said. "Your throat is all cut."

"How do you feed me?"

"Through a vein in your arm. We use a tube."

"Eight dollars a day," he moaned. "Well, I'm going to eat something. I'm going to get my money's worth." Then to the nurse, "Bring me a glassful of tea."

"All right. I'll make some tea for you."

She left the room, returned shortly with the tea and injected it into the vein of his arm.

"Yoi, yoi, yoi," he wailed.

"What's the matter?" she asked. "Too hot?"

"No. Too sweet. Put some lemon in!" **LAURIE, JR.**

## 46

Elmer Smudgegegunk was married to an old shrew, one of those women that's always nagging and raising the devil around the house. At times, she even went so far as to throw pots and pans at Elmer's bean. The poor guy stood it as long as he could, then decided to find a little consolation via the liquor route, so, for one whole week, he went on a binge. Every night, he'd return home as blind as a bat. He became a chronic lush and was plastered day and night, which worried his friends down at the grocery store, so they decided to do something to cure him. The plan was for one of them to dress up all in red like a devil, with horns on, and carry a pitchfork. The self-appointed benefactor hid in the cemetery, which he knew Elmer would have to pass on his way home. It was midnight when poor Elmer staggered by the cemetery. As he passed a tombstone, the devil jumped up from behind it. Elmer stopped, and gazed at him, as he swayed unsteadily on his feet.

"You'll have to stop drinking!" warned the devil.

"Who are you?" asked Elmer, thick-tongued.

"I'm the devil!"

"Oh, you're the devil," laughed Elmer boisterously. "I'm glad to meet you! I married a sister of yours!"  FORD

## 47

When I went to work for Metro Goldwyn Mayer, a young couple got on a train which was en route to the Coast. A fellow seated opposite spotted them as newlyweds on a honeymoon because they still had rice on their apparel. But they looked sad—very sad! After a while, both started to cry. The next day, it was the same—they were still crying. It was really tragic! The fellow who was observing them figured that maybe both realized their mistake—that she had married the wrong man, and he, the wrong girl. Naturally, he hesitated about intruding or asking questions, but the following day, when he found them both still in tears, he was unable to control his sympathy. He wanted to be of assistance. So, he said:

"Pardon me, folks. I don't want to butt in, but I know you are newlyweds, and it's apparent that a great tragedy has happened to you."

"Yes," sobbed the groom, unable to stop the flow of tears, "for three days now, we've been on the wrong train!"

HERSHFIELD

## 48

Two fellows went out hunting for the first time. As they prowled through the dense woods looking for game, they became separated. As darkness descended, one fellow, Barney Rabinowitz, got lost. Panic-stricken, he began to holler:

"Man in the woods is lost! Man in the woods is lost!"

"Who?" hooted an owl from a tree top.

"Barney Rabinowitz!" answered the lost one.

"Who?" hooted the owl again.

"Barney Rabinowitz, from the Bronx, New York!"

"Who?" repeated the owl.

"Never mind!" said the annoyed Barney. "I'll find my way out myself!"

LAURIE, JR.

## 49

At the last Army and Navy Ball in Washington, Paul McNutt told me this story.

One very dark night, on the extreme outskirts of an Army camp, a rookie sentry was on duty. Suddenly, he was startled by the sound of horses' hooves. The rookie sentry challenged:

"Who goes there?" he called.

"Regimental Commander!" came a voice out of the darkness.

"All right, Colonel. Dismount, advance, and be recognized!"

The Colonel got off his horse. He walked over to the rookie. "O.K., Colonel," he said. "Proceed!"

The Colonel remounted, started away, then as a thought struck him, turned and addressed the rookie again.

"By the way," he asked, "who posted you away out here?"

"Nobody," exclaimed the rookie, "I'm just practicing!"

FORD

## 50

A hillbilly brought a fellow into Court after a fight.

"Tell your story!" demanded the Judge.

"Well, I was in a telephone booth talking to my gal, proposing marriage," exclaimed the hillbilly, "when a guy suddenly wants to use the telephone. He opens the door, grabs me by the neck and throws me out of the booth!"

"Then you got angry?" asked the Judge.

"Yes, but I got real sore when he grabbed my gal and threw her out, too!" HERSHFIELD

## 51

Bloomberg was telling about a dream he had.

"Last night, I was dreaming," he began. "I dreamt that I went to the Beaver Street Pharmacy. I went in and said, 'Give me a razor blade.' 'That will be seventy-five cents,' said the Boss. So, I gave him a dollar bill and he went over to the cash register, rings up the seventy-five cents, then started talking to another customer, forgetting all about my change. So, I said to myself, 'Bloomberg, but how do you know you are dreaming?' And I answered, 'Listen, if I wasn't dreaming, would I let him charge me seventy-five cents for a razor blade?"

LAURIE, JR.

## 52

In the olden days, in the middle west, a fellow by the name of Monohan was working as a pick-and-shovel laborer for a railroad. Raised in the west, he had never been near any waterways. On his first vacation in twenty years, he went to the Atlantic Seaboard for a visit. For the first time in his life, he saw a huge anchor hanging from the bow of an ocean liner. It started Monohan talking to himself.

"I don't believe it," he muttered. "There ain't a man in the world who could swing that pick!"

FORD

## 53

In the old days, when Eddie Rickenbacker was an automobile salesman, he tried to sell a moron a car.

"Is it a good car?" asked the gooferoo.

"A swell car," assured the salesman.

"Is it fast?"

"Very fast," replied the salesman. "In fact, if you got in this car at eight o'clock at night, you'd be in Brooklyn at four in the morning!"

"I'll think it over," said the mental delinquent, and left.

The next day, he entered the place again and collared the salesman.

"I don't want the car," he said, "because all night long I racked my brains and I can't think of one single reason why I should be in Brooklyn at four o'clock in the morning!"

HERSHFIELD

**54**

Doyle and Ginnis, a couple of laborers, were working on a job out in the country.

"Why don't you knock off work?" suggested Ginnis. "You live near here."

"I don't want to go home," replied Doyle, "it's too early."

"The foreman's gone," reminded Ginnis, "so you might as well go home."

"I think I will surprise my wife!" declared Doyle.

So he left. In a short while he came dashing back—all out of breath.

"What's the matter?" asked Ginnis.

"I wanted to surprise my wife," explained Doyle, gasping for breath, "so I sneaked on the front porch, peeked into the window, and who do you think was sitting on the sofa hugging and kissing my wife?—the foreman!"

"*Our* foreman was sitting on the sofa hugging and kissing your wife?" said the amazed Ginnis. "What did you do?"

"I sneaked away on my tiptoes and ran back here," he confessed, wiping beads of perspiration from his brow. "That sure was a close shave—he nearly caught me!"

LAURIE, JR.

**55**

One night, after making a speech at the Illinois Athletic Club in Chicago, I went to a party that was held in a three-story house. There was something doing on every floor. On the top one, a roulette wheel was spinning. On the second, they were spinning the bottle, and on the first floor, they were just—spinning! Invitations sent out announced it was a Dutch Treat party. One was sent to François Le Blanc, a

Frenchman. Another was sent to Sandy MacTavish, a Scotch-man, and one was sent to Sam Goldfarb, a Bronxman. As everyone knows, at a Dutch Treat, one has to bring some-thing along. So, the Frenchman brought wine, the Bronxman brought salami, and the Scotchman brought—his brother!

FORD

**56**

Down South, in the old prohibition days, a colored Deacon called a member of his congregation aside.

"Ah wants to give a big party fo' mah congregation," confided the Deacon. "Of course, ah doan want to disobey the law, but Ah thinks it would be a little livelier with the 'stuff'—but where we-all goin' to get it?"

"You-all has a right to get it because you-all is a Deacon," declared the member. "You-all can get a permit for sacra-mental wine. All you-all has to do is go and ask for it."

The Deacon followed his advice, secured the permit, then went to the place where the sacramental wine was dispensed.

"Ah has a permit for sacramental wine," informed the Deacon. "Ah'd like to get some."

"What kind of sacramental wine do you want?" asked the dispenser.

"In consideration of the congregation's decision—gin!"

HERSHFIELD

**57**

Joe V. Connolly, head of King Features, told this story at a Banshee Luncheon at the Waldorf-Astoria.

A colored girl went to the office of an editor of a news-paper in Louisville, Ky.

"Mah husband died," she explained, "an' Ah'd like to put in one of those notices in the paper."

"You mean an obituary?" asked the editor.

"Yeah, Ah guess that's what you-all calls them. How much are they?"

"We charge fifty cents an inch."

"Oh, Ah can't pay that kind of money," gasped the sepia one. "That man of mine was over six foot tall!"

LAURIE, JR.

## 58

A young colored fellow who was a door attendant in an apartment house got a "surprise" one morning in the mail. It was a greeting card from Uncle Sam which assured him his induction was due. So he quickly got in touch with his pal to discuss it.

"Which branch of the service does you-all craves to enter?" queried the pal.

"Well, Ah doan see no reason why Ah should change," answered the elected one, after deep thought. "You see, Ah got a lot of experience as a door-tender, so Ah can be a door-tender in the heavy artillery."

"What does you-all mean—a door-tender in the heavy artillery?"

"You-all know that little door in the hind end of a cannon?"

"Yeah. What about it?"

"Well, Ah can open that door, put in a shell, close the door, aim the cannon, pull the trigger, the cannon speaks its piece, then all Ah have to say is—'Tojo, count yo' soldiers'!"

FORD

**59**

A woman entered a butcher shop and called the boss aside.

"I know what conditions are today," she said, "but do you think I can get fifty pounds of beef?"

"Certainly," he replied.

He wrapped up the amount requested.

"When will you send it?" she asked.

"I can't send it," he said. "You know what conditions are today. Furthermore, I have no way of delivering it."

"Why?" said the woman in surprise. "Your wagon is out in front of the store."

"But you have the horse!" he informed.      HERSHFIELD

**60**

A Scotchman was outside of a liquor store, studying the bottles in the window. Suddenly he spotted one marked "one cent," so he entered the place.

"I want that bottle in the window," he said, indicating the one that attracted his attention.

"Yes, sir," replied the proprietor, and got it for him. After he wrapped it up, the Scotchman paid him—one penny.

"A penny? You're crazy, aren't you?" remarked the proprietor.

"It's marked 'one cent,'" argued the canny one.

"Oh," laughed the proprietor, beginning to understand. "That numeral happened to fall down from the bottle above marked 'four ninety-one' and you thought it was 'one cent' for this bottle."

"It's marked 'one cent,'" insisted the Scotchman, "and you've got to sell it to me for 'one cent.'"

"You're crazy, man," said the proprietor, annoyed. "If you don't stop that stuff, I'll call a cop!"

"Go ahead!"

He did.

"What's the matter?" asked the custodian of the law.

Both sides were told. The policeman told the proprietor that he had to sell it for the penny. Finally, in disgust, and to stop further argument, the proprietor sold the bottle of liquor for—one cent! The following day the cop met the canny Scot on the street.

"How are you, Scotty?" he said. "Gee, I had to laugh yesterday when I made that fellow sell you that bottle of liquor for 'one cent.' Oh," he continued, unable to suppress his laughter, "I'll never be able to forget the look on that guy's face!"

"Huh!" sniffed the Scotchman. "You think the look on his face yesterday was funny? You should have seen the look on his face this morning when I tried to get two cents back for the bottle!"

LAURIE, JR.

## 61

After a week's vacation in a summer hotel, the clerk handed the guest a bill for thirty-five dollars.

"Thirty-five dollars for a room in this old hotel?" asked the guest, indignantly.

"Thirty-five dollars includes meals," explained the clerk courteously.

"But I didn't eat here," explained the guest.

"That's not my fault," assured the clerk. "They were here for you."

"In that case," declared the guest, "you owe me thirty-five dollars for kissing my wife."

"What do you mean," flared the clerk. "I didn't kiss your wife!"

"It's your own fault," said the guest. "She was here for you!"                                                   FORD

## 62

One day a wife overheard her husband phoning his office.

"Yes, Toots—don't worry, Toots," he said. "Everything will be all right, Toots—yes, Toots—okay, Toots—all right, Toots—good-by, Toots."

After he hung up, his wife sauntered into the room.

"What goes on?" she asked.

"I was calling the office," he explained.

"After all these years you're suddenly calling your stenographer Molly 'Toots'?" she asked, frigidly.

"No," informed the husband, "I say 'Toots' for short. Molly is on her vacation. This is a substi-'toots'!"

                                                   HERSHFIELD

## 63

When Spyrous Skouras, president of Twentieth Century-Fox Studios, showed me around the lot, he told me this story.

Two sons of Greece met on the lower East Side of New York.

"Hey, Potisgaloup," called one. "What's a polar bear?"

"Oh, a polar bear," the other informed, "he sits on ice all day and eats-a the fish."

"I won't do it!"

"You won't do what?"

"A friend of mine died and his-a wife wants-a me to be a 'polar bear'!"                                    LAURIE, JR.

**64**

Screwball Jake had a sister by the name of Beansie, who had a lot of boll weevil in her hay loft. Beansie also had a boy friend. One day he took her to an art exhibit. They came to a painting of "The Spirit of Seventy-Six."

"You know," explained the boy friend, "them's the original Yankees!"

"Really?" said the enlightened Beansie. "Which one is Babe Ruth?"                                                                FORD

**65**

At the opening of Belmont Park, Tim Mara was relating the experience a friend of his had on a recent trip to Miami.

"Oh, did I have trouble with my wife!" he groaned. "She's one of those fancy ladies who's never satisfied. She had to go to a hotel that charges forty dollars a day for a room, so we got a room for forty dollars a day! The next afternoon she had to go out horseback riding. Right away she fell off the horse and got knocked unconscious! I called a doctor and he said she'd be unconscious for twelve weeks!"

"Unconscious for twelve weeks?" gasped a friend who had listened patiently. "What did you do?"

"I moved to a cheaper hotel!"                                        HERSHFIELD

**66**

One moonlight night, after a Prom dance, a fellow begged to drive a beautiful young girl home. She accepted and got in his little roadster. As they were driving along he sighed deeply.

"You're beautiful!" he murmured audibly. "That golden hair!"

"Thank you," she answered.

"And your big blue eyes! They're beautiful, too!"

"Thank you."

"And your lips—and pearly teeth!"

She again thanked him. As they rode along he continued to shower her with compliments, but she remained silent. Suddenly she spoke.

"Can you drive with one hand?" she asked, softly.

"Sure!" he quickly replied, hopefully.

"Well," she suggested, "wipe your nose—it's running!"

LAURIE, JR.

## 67

Neither McGuire nor Casey could tell time and both were wise to each other. One day Casey found out that McGuire had bought himself a watch. To get a rise out of him he decided to kid him about it.

"Mac," he began, "what time is it by your watch?"

"There she is," said McGuire, pulling out his watch and showing it to him.

"Darned if she ain't!" admitted the stymied Casey.

FORD

## 68

While having lunch with Louis B. Mayer and Louella Parsons at the Brown Derby in Beverly Hills, this gag came up:

Beautiful Hedy Lamarr wanted to go hunting for big game—bears—so a fellow gave her some advice. He told her that if anyone goes bear hunting he must be sure to watch the bear carefully in the distance, because if a bear sees a human being he gets up on his hind legs and stands up. In a situation like that the best thing to do is to motion for the bear to come forward—and he will. So beautiful Hedy went out into the woods hunting. Late in the afternoon she saw a bear and, remembering the advice, began motioning to the bear to come forward. As he started toward her she lifted her rifle and took aim, but before she could shoot the bear grabbed her and started to crush the beautiful one in his arms! They wrestled around a short while but after a herculean effort she managed to free herself and succeeded in running away. But—she wanted to get that bear! So, the next morning, bright and early, she again went out into the woods hunting for him. Lo and behold, she saw the same bear in the same place, but the minute he saw her he began making a motion for her to come over to him!

HERSHFIELD

## 69

Max Bloomberg and Sam Epstein had a reunion. They hadn't seen each other for a very long time.

"Max!" enthused Sam. "Oi! Am I glad to see you! I haven't seen you in twenty-five years!"

"That's right," said Max, beaming.

"Oh, what a boy you used to be," reminisced Sam. "You used to play cards, drink and smoke and chase around! You know, you used to be a bummer, no? What's happened to you since I saw you last?"

"I'm married," said Max. "I've got a family."

"You got children?" asked the dubious Sam.

"Yes," assured Max. "I got children. Two sons."

"Boys?" asked Sam.

"Yes," informed Max. "I've got one boy who makes me

a lot of trouble—a lot of it. You see, he's at that uncertain age—between twenty-five and thirty-five. He drinks, he smokes, and to tell you the truth, Sam—he's a bum!"

"How's the other boy?" asked Sam.

"The other boy takes after me," replied Max.

"Is that so?" said Sam, sympathetically. "Three bums in one family!"                                           LAURIE, JR.

## 70

Two tonsils lived in a drunk's throat.

"Hey, where are we?" asked one tonsil.

"We must be in Capistrano," answered the other. "Here comes another swallow!"                                    FORD

## 71

T. Cottington Rappaport was a decent sort of a chap and worked hard. He became very successful and somebody proposed him for membership at a very swank club which boasted mostly bluebloods. The membership committee put Rappaport through a third degree of questions.

"Did your parents come from Russia?" he was asked.

"No," answered T. Cottington.

Although one member of the board was skeptical, Rappaport was accepted in the club. A few weeks later, after an investigation, he was ordered to appear before the committee again, as charges had been preferred against him.

"Why did you lie to us?" the spokesman inquired. "We asked you if your parents came from Russia and you said 'no.'"

"They didn't," answered Rappaport. "They're still there!"

HERSHFIELD

**72**

Two East Side girls met on the street.

"I heard you were at a party last night."

"Yes. A masquerade party."

"What happened?"

"Choo Choo Rabinowitz came all dressed up as Carmen. She even had a rose between her teeth. And Jerkimer Cohen, he was dressed as a matador."

"Is that something like a cuspidor?"

"No."

"What happened?"

"As Jerkimer passed by Choo Choo, he began to tease her, so she got mad and threw her rose at him!"

"Well, what happened?"

"Jerkimer picked up the rose and threw her teeth back at her!"                                                LAURIE, JR.

**73**

I read in the newspapers where Mrs. Roosevelt said that housewives should be paid a weekly salary. She said, "Any housewife who stays at home maintains a household." But I don't know how she found out. Anyway, the article leads me to believe that eventually we'll have a housewives' union and I just want to see what happens when the housewives go out on strike and the strike breakers come in and take their places!                                                FORD

**74**

I. J. Fox was invited by a very ritzy woman who was giving a very exclusive party at her Long Island mansion. She had to engage an extra butler for the occasion. Everyone knows what the servant problem is these days, so she had to be satisfied with what she could get. When her guests arrived, she was the perfect hostess, doing everything in a very ultra and ritzy manner. At the buffet supper, she was carrying her plate of food when an accident occurred—she dropped a deviled egg.

"Oh, servant," she called, not knowing the new butler's name, "I just dropped an egg. What shall I do?"

"Cackle, toots, cackle!"          HERSHFIELD

## 75

A couple checked into a hotel. After cleaning up, the lady forgot to turn off the faucets in the bathroom. About a half-hour later the guest in the room directly under them opened his window, stuck out his head and hollered upstairs to attract their attention.

"Hey, you up there!" he shouted.

The fellow upstairs opened his window and stuck out his head.

"What's the matter?" he asked.

"Turn off those faucets in your bathroom!" he demanded. "It's pouring down here! What's the matter with you?"

He climaxed his bitter denunciation with a wild outburst of profanity that was shocking.

"Wait a minute! Hey, wait a minute!" advised the man upstairs. "Stop your cursing—I've got a lady up here!"

"What do you think I've got down here," yowled the irate one, "a duck?"          LAURIE, JR.

## 76

A man and his wife got into one of those knock-down drag-out arguments.

"You brute!" she cried. "Before we were married you told me you were well off!"

"I was!" he snapped, "but I didn't know it!" FORD

## 77

Bill Robinson told me this story the night Commissioner Moss gave him a citation for playing more Benefits than any other performer on Broadway.

A woman who couldn't sleep tried everything from counting sheep to every form of medicine. A friend told her worried husband that a singing canary might be the remedy. One that could sing beautifully—it would soothe her. In desperation, the husband went to a bird shop where they auction off hundreds and hundreds of birds every week. He selected a singing one, purchased it, and took it home to his wife. That night it sang beautifully, and for the first time in ages his wife got a good night's sleep. In the morning, she was very happy and her husband was thrilled. In thanking the bird for singing his wife to sleep, he noticed for the first time that the canary had only—one leg! So he grabbed the bird and dashed back to the bird shop.

"Look!" he remonstrated. "You gave me a bird with one leg!"

"Make up your mind," was the curt reply. "Do you want a singer or a dancer?" HERSHFIELD

## 78

A salesman, traveling in the Ozarks, met a character called Zeke, and engaged him in conversation.

"Zeke, is that your boy, there?" he asked indicating a tall, lanky-legged kid with ill-fitting clothes.

"Yes, sir," replied Zeke, "that's my son, Lem."

"Lem's quite a big boy. How old is he?"

"Well, he's about fourteen years old, I guess."

"What's he going to do—stay around these parts?"

"Yes. Just like we all did."

"Why don't you send Lem to the city and give him an education, so when he grows up, he'll learn something?"

"I don't know."

"I have a friend who has a little store in New York City —up in the Bronx. He'll give Lem a job, then he can go to school nights and learn something."

"Guess you're right," replied Zeke, "maybe he should get a little education."

So arrangements were made, and Lem went to New York City.

"Zeke. I think you made a big mistake," predicted the spokesman for his neighbors. "Lem ain't gonna be our folks any more. He ain't gonna be a hillbilly any more. He's gonna change in that great big city!"

When all agreed with the spokesman, Zeke began to worry. Three years later, Lem returned home to the Ozarks for a visit. His father was still worried as he waited for him at the railroad station—hoping he hadn't changed. The train pulled in and Lem got off. Zeke greeted him.

"Lem, tell me the truth," said the worried Zeke, "did you change?"

"No, Papa," replied Lem in strong Jewish dialect, "once a hillbilly—always a hillbilly!"                LAURIE, JR.

## 79

Al Schacht, baseball's clown prince, came home from business one evening feeling very glum.

"What's the matter with you?" asked his brother.

"I was in my restaurant this noon, and I had an argument with a waiter," he explained. "He insulted me. He called me a pig!"

"Listen," said the brother, "with the price of pork what it is today, you don't have to feel so insulted!"            FORD

## 80

There's a sign in front of a store and on it is lettered the name S. Cartwright. A very ritzy dame, the dowager type, passed, saw the sign, stopped and muttered to herself, "Cartwright—Cartwright! I wonder if they are THE Cartwrights." To satisfy her curiosity, she entered the store.

"Are you of the Boston Cartwrights?" she inquired.

"No," informed the proprietor, "the Boston Cartwrights are the Epsteins—we're the Ginsbergs!"            HERSHFIELD

## 81

Mrs. Polakoff met Mrs. Weinberg in the grocery store.

"How's your son Montgomery?" inquired Mrs. Weinberg.

"Oh, he's in the Army," replied Mrs. Polakoff.

"He was taken?"

"A couple of days ago."

"What is he doing in the Army?"

"He's a Keep Out."

"A what?"

"A Keep Out! He's a Keep Out!"

"I never heard of such a thing. Is that a Colonel?"

"No. He's a Keep Out."

"What do you mean, a Keep Out?"

"Private—Private—Keep out!"            LAURIE, JR.

**82**

A couple of draftees returned to their home in the country on a furlough. To celebrate the occasion, their father went out in the barnyard and killed a couple of chickens. Mother cooked them and the boys ate every bit—right down to the bones! After dinner, they ·went out to the barnyard. The rooster began crowing.

"What's that rooster crowing for at this time of the day?" one asked his father.

"Well, he knows where those chickens went," explained his father, "and he's proud that he's got two sons in the Army!" FORD

**83**

A man went into Lindy's, sat down and studied the menu. The waiter came for his order.

"What!" exclaimed the customer, "you charge one dollar for a veal cutlet here?"

"That's what we charge here," assured the waiter, nonchalantly.

"The restaurant across the street only charges seventy-five cents for a veal cutlet," informed the customer.

"Then why don't you eat in the restaurant across the street?" suggested the waiter.

"They're all out of veal cutlets," was the reply.

"Listen, when we're out of veal cutlets," confided the waiter, "we only charge seventy-five cents, too!"

HERSHFIELD

**84**

A stranger came to a small town and went into Schultz's Baker Shop. "Can you make me two hundred doughnuts?" he asked.

"Yes," assured Schultz, "but it will take three or four hours."

"O. K. I'll be back later for them."

The stranger left, went across the street into a tailor shop and selected a swell, ready-made suit of clothes for one hundred dollars.

"I want you to charge it," he said.

"Charge it?" replied the surprised tailor. "I don't even know you. You're a stranger in town, aren't you?"

"Sure."

"Do you know anybody in town?"

"Yes," replied the stranger, "I know the baker across the street."

They went outside, just as the baker was coming out of his shop. "You say you know him?"

"I know him very well."

Suddenly the stranger got an idea.

"Mr. Schultz!" he called, "how about that two hundred?"

"I'll have it for you late this afternoon!" Schultz hollered back.

"Give him a hundred," he ordered, indicating the tailor.

"O. K.," said Schultz.

"Go ahead," apologized the convinced tailor. "Take the suit!"                                          LAURIE, JR.

## 85

Ditsey Baumwortle was a barber once. He wasn't more than a little shaver when a customer walked in one day and got into the barber's chair. "I want a shave and don't you cut me!" warned the customer.

"Don't worry! If I cut you, I'll give you ten cents,"

promised Ditsey, "and would you believe it, the customer ahead of you went out of here eighty cents to the good!"

FORD

## 86

Henpecked Clancy was deathly afraid of his wife and everyone knew it. Some blackmailers heard about it.

"We'll frame this Clancy guy," said one; "he's afraid of his wife and he's got dough."

For the first time in his life, Clancy's wife permitted him to go to the beach without her. The blackmailers found out about it and framed with a beautiful blonde to flirt with him so they could snap pictures to further their scheme. Everything worked out as planned, and the blackmailers succeeded in getting different poses of Clancy and the blonde, on the beach—playing leapfrog—sitting on each other's lap—under the boardwalk and in other compromising positions. Naturally, Clancy was unaware of it.

A few days later, the blackmailers came to his office figuring on scaring him into paying off, and showed him prints of the different pictures they had snapped. Clancy studied each and every one.

"They're marvelous," he beamed. "I'll take a dozen of each!"

HERSHFIELD

## 87

Two men were talking about a mutual friend named Smitty.

"Poor Smitty," said one, "he's terribly henpecked."

"He can't go out with the boys or have any fun," said the other, "it's really awful."

"Let's go over and see the poor guy tonight," suggested the first one.

The other agreed. So, that night they went over to visit Smitty.

When they got to the front door of his house, they were surprised to hear his voice raised in anger. They stopped and listened: "Shut up! I'll tell you who's boss in this house—I'm boss!" he raved. "Not a word now—I'm through being henpecked! Sit down or I'll slap you down!"

"Smitty's finally asserted himself," whispered one of the delighted listeners.

"Let's ring the bell and go in," enthused the other, gleefully.

The doorbell was rung, and Smitty appeared.

"Hello, fellows," he said, warmly. "Gee, I'm so glad you came over—I'm so lonesome."

"Isn't your wife with you?" asked one, puzzled.

"No," Smitty informed. "She went away on a vacation two weeks ago. I'm all alone in the house, so I was just rehearsing what I should have said to her years ago when I first got married!"

LAURIE, JR.

## 88

There's a smart-cracking waiter in a restaurant where I usually go. One noon, I took two friends there for lunch. One ordered fried eggs, the other scrambled eggs, and I ordered a boiled egg. The waiter jotted down the order, then looked up with a fiendish grin.

"You know 'Senator,'" he cracked, "this order reminds me of your Saturday Night Broadcast!"

FORD

**89**

Business wasn't going so good for Sam and he looked it. One day, he came home from work, and much to his annoyance, saw his wife sporting a new dress.

"What, another new dress?" he raved. "Every day, it's another new dress! I can't afford it! Look at me, working like a slave and you're buying new dresses!"

"It's your own fault, Sam," she said, "because wherever I go—at every party—every affair, they say, 'There goes Sam's wife—look how she's dressed'!"

"For Heaven's sake," he ranted, "look how I'm dressed— and I'm Sam!"                                                 HERSHFIELD

**90**

Jake was trying to pull a little pony along a road, but the pony wouldn't move. A fellow passed by, then stopped.

"Can I help you?" asked the stranger.

"Yes. Please give my horsie a little push."

He obliged. The pony moved a bit, then stopped again. So, the stranger helped him some more, pushing the pony up to the fence which surrounded Jake's house.

"Thank you very much," said Jake, "but if you don't mind, would you push him through the gate for me?"

"Sure. I've got nothing else to do."

So, he obliged again.

"You've got nothing else to do?" asked Jake. "Then please push him through the front door so I can take him into my house."

He did.

"Please. Just a few more minutes," was Jake's request. "Help me up the stairs with him."

The stranger pushed the pony up the stairs to the second floor.

"Now one more push into the bathtub!"

The request was granted. By now, the curiosity of the good samaritan was aroused.

"What's this all about?" he asked.

"I've got a brother-in-law who's a smarty," explained Jake. "And every time he comes home from work, I try to tell him something I know or saw but he never lets me finish and always says, 'Yeah, I know—I know—I know,' so, tonight, when he comes home and goes upstairs to wash his hands in the bathroom, he'll see the pony and will come down and say, 'Jake! Do you know there's a pony in the bathroom?' and I'll say, 'Yeah, I know—I know—I know'!"

LAURIE, JR.

## 91

Jack Dempsey told me this story one night between fights at Madison Square Garden.

A fellow by the name of Hogan was once asked to referee the main bout between Finnegan, who was a friend of his, and a fellow by the name of Schultz, whom Hogan didn't like very well. In the first round, Schultz wound up a haymaker, hit Finnegan on the button, and down he went! Hogan sauntered over to Finnegan's prostrate form and slowly started counting over him.

"One, two, Finnegan get up!" he said. "Three, four, Finnegan, if I wasn't a friend of yours, I'd kick you in the ribs! —four, five, Finnegan, you're no use to the community, or the Fifth Ward, or to your family to let a Dutchman like him knock you down! Five, six——"

By that time, Finnegan's head cleared, and he got up. He started one, right from the floor, which landed smack on Schultz's kisser, and down he went! Hogan quickly dashed over and began rapidly counting.

"One, two, three, four, five—five and five are ten! You're out!—you bum!"          FORD

## 92

A young draftee was shipped to Africa. He was put in the camel brigade which was assigned to desert duty. For hours, he was riding along over the hot sand in the terrific heat. All of a sudden, the draftee got off the camel, disrobed down to his B.V.D.'s and started running.

"Where are you going?" shouted the Corporal.

The draftee stopped.

"I'm going in the water for a swim," the draftee explained.

"There's no water around for three hundred miles!" exclaimed the Corporal.

"That's a shame," said the draftee, "with such a wonderful beach like this!"          HERSHFIELD

## 93

A fellow went over on the East Side to Sammy's Delicatessen Store. "Give me three pickles," he said. Sammy grabbed the pickles. "And a pound of corn beef." Sammy cut it, grabbed the meat with his hands, weighed it, then wrapped it up.

"Wait a minute," said the annoyed customer, "I don't want any of that!"

"What's the matter?" asked Sammy.

"You're grabbing everything with your dirty hands. I don't like that. Keep the stuff!"

Indignantly, he walked out of the place.

A month later, he passed by Sammy's place and was amazed at the change. It was all repainted white and had a new sign—"Sammy's Sanitary Clean Delicatessen Store." The fellow was so impressed by the immaculate appearance of everything, that he couldn't resist going in. There was Sammy, wearing a spotless white hat, white coat and white apron!

"Give me three pickles," said the fellow.

"Pardon me," said Sammy, "but aren't you the man that was here a few weeks ago?"

"Yes."

"Weren't you complaining about the fingers?"

"Yes."

"Well, you see the place now," Sammy boasted, "everything's perfect — neat — spick-and-span. I'm working with gloves now. When you ask for pickles, I use a fork—no fingers! When you ask for corned beef, I use a fork—no fingers! Everything's with a fork—nothing handled with my fingers! Do you see this handkerchief in my pocket? When I want to blow my nose, I don't touch it with my fingers— I pull a string—this little one—and out comes the handkerchief!"

"What do you do to put it back?" inquired the interested customer.

"Use a fork!" said Sammy.                    LAURIE, JR.

## 94

Mrs. Wookle, a big fat dame, is the chief boss of all she surveys, including her little shrimp husband, Wellington,

who married her in a not too lucid moment. Mrs. Wookle
is so painfully neat around the house that she makes life
miserable for the little weasel, in fact she makes him take
off his shoes before he enters the house for fear he'll track
dirt into the rooms. One night, he came home from work,
and found her in an unusually angry mood.

"Wellington, I found a grease spot on one of the dining-
room chairs and I think it came off the pants that you wear
at the factory," she bellowed. "Now, something's got to be
done about it!"

"Look here, Sarah," he piped weakly, trying to appear
brave, "for fifteen years, I've been taking my shoes off before I came into this house and that's as far as I'm going to
go. And, grease spot or no grease spot—no pants off!"

FORD

## 95

At the Editors and Publishers convention at the Waldorf,
Bill Hearst, Jr., told this nifty.

An editor of a newspaper heard that a woman died who
was married sixty years to the same man. Thinking it a good
human-interest story, he assigned a sob sister and a cameraman to cover it, with instructions to get a picture of the
bereaved husband, Ivan Petrovsky, looking at his wife's
photo. So the sob sister and cameraman went to Petrovsky's
home, and the servant who answered the doorbell informed
them he was in the library but warned he really shouldn't
be disturbed. They promised not to, and tiptoed in. As they
opened the door to the library, they saw Petrovsky in an
easy chair with the maid sitting on his lap. He had his arms
around her.

"We're amazed, Mr. Petrovsky!" exclaimed the sob sister, "especially after sixty years. Your wife just died!"

"In my grief," he alibied, "I should know what I'm doing?"

HERSHFIELD

## 96

A Scotchman came into a barber shop.

"How much do you charge for a haircut?" he asked.

"Fifty cents," answered the barber.

"How much do you charge for a shave?"

"Ten cents."

"All right," said the Scotchman, "shave my head."

LAURIE, JR.

## 97

Dugan was haled into court for committing modified mayhem on a fellow man.

"Dugan, what have you got to say for committing assault and battery on this man here?" coldly asked the judge as he indicated the victim.

"I was laconic," was Dugan's alibi.

"Do you know what laconic means?" queried his Honor.

"No, I don't," admitted Dugan, "but I gave him a rap on the side of the snoot to be on the safe side!" FORD

## 98

Giuseppi, the barber, suspected a fellow in the neighborhood, named Sammy, of running around with his best girl, and figured that some day he would come into his shop and he'd get revenge. Sure enough, one day Sammy came in for a shave. After he got into the chair, Giuseppi grabbed the unsuspecting one by the throat, and held a razor menacingly over him.

"You're running around with my girl," he hissed. "I'll kill you!"

Sammy was frightened stiff.

"Let me say just two words," he pleaded.

"No! You cannot steal my girl and get away with it!" He began swinging the razor dangerously near his Adam's apple.

"Please, let me say just two words," repeated Sammy, weakly.

"No!" screamed the now-enraged barber, "you cannot do this to me!"

"Let me say two words," gasped Sammy.

"All right!" agreed the temperamental one. "What?"

"Let go!"                                 HERSHFIELD

## 99

Bloomberg escaped from a concentration camp in Germany and was being hunted by a Storm Trooper, so, in the darkness of the night, he went to a friend who owned a toy shop.

"You've got to hide me!" pleaded Bloomberg. "A Storm Trooper is after me!"

"Here's a big bag that has bells in it," said the friend, "get in it."

"What about the bells?" asked the cautious Bloomberg.

"I'll take them out." Which he did. Then he put Bloomberg in the bag and tied it up.

"Be very quiet now!" he warned.

The words were barely out of his mouth when the Storm Trooper entered.

"Did you see a little fellow named Bloomberg?" he demanded.

"No, I didn't see anybody."

"Are you sure you didn't hide him in your shop?"

"I didn't see anybody."

The Storm Trooper made a rapid search of the place.

"What's in that bag there?" he asked, suspiciously.

"Bells!"

The Storm Trooper hit it with the butt end of his gun.

"Ting-a-linga-ling-a-ling," chimed Bloomberg in his best imitation.                                                    LAURIE, JR.

## 100

One stormy night, a guy called Dopey was on his hands and knees on the corner of Fifty-fourth Street and Fifth Avenue. Apparently, he was searching for something. A cop came along.

"Did you lose something, Buddy?" the cop inquired.

"Yeah," said Dopey. "I lost a half-dollar on Sixth Avenue."

"If you lost a half-dollar on Sixth Avenue," asked the cop, "why are you looking for it here on Fifth Avenue?"

"Because there's more light here!" informed the Dopey one.                                                         FORD

## 101

A colored fellow who lived down South and had never left that territory since birth, got a job up North. He arrived in the city in below-zero weather—in the worst blizzard of the winter. It was so cold, that he got blue, stiffened up and froze to death! Unable to identify him, the city authorities decided to cremate him. They put him in the oven of the crematory and waited one hour before examining his last remains. Then, the attendant opened the oven door.

"Close that door!" called the voice of the colored fellow, "Ah feels a draft!"        HERSHFIELD

## 102

A favorite story told to me by Alfred J. McCosker, Chairman of the Board of the Mutual Broadcasting Company and President of WOR.

Two moron hillbillys, named Lem and Bud, had never seen or heard a radio. Their first introduction to one was on an evening when a commentator was discussing the mental delinquency and ignorance of certain natives who live in the Ozarks.

"That's terrible," commented Lem, "that man talking like that about our people. I'm not goin' to let him say that!" So he took his shotgun, blasted away at the radio—and it stopped.

Next day, the two morons came over to see the radio again, as organ music was being broadcasted.

"Hey, Lem!" called Bud.

"What is it?"

"You know the man you shot last night?"

"Yeah."

"Well, they're burying him today."        LAURIE, JR.

## 103

Up in my home town, there's a miserly old farmer who makes his wife keep a weekly account of every penny she spends on herself. At the end of each week, he carefully examines it with groans, growls and grumbles. One time, he was going over the account with the usual unsuppressed emotions.

"Sarah!" he called to his wife. "Do you think I'm made of money? You spent fifty cents for corn plasters, twenty cents for aspirin and three dollars to have two teeth pulled! That's three dollars and seventy cents you spent this week on your own personal pleasure!"                                    FORD

## 104

Buck Crouse, partner of Howard Lindsey, told this story at the last Mayfair party.

A moron had never been to a theater before in his life, so he had to be told where the theater was, how to find the box office, and how to buy a ticket. After he bought one, he still was in a quandary.

"Now where do I go?" he asked.

"Through that door there," the man at the box office replied, indicating the front door of the theater. The piece of chipped china went in and in a few minutes returned.

"I want to buy another ticket," he said. After getting one, he entered the theater and again returned. After buying another ticket and returning for still another, the box-office man stopped him.

"Just a minute," he said. "You've bought three tickets already. What's the matter?"

"Every time I go through that door," complained the moron, "and give a fellow my ticket—he tears it up!"

                                                            HERSHFIELD

## 105

Two fellows were discussing another.

"How's this fellow Bloomberg?" asked one. "Has he got money?"

"Oh, yes," assured the other. "He must be very, very wealthy."

"What makes you think so?"

"Well, I'll tell you. He saves five hundred dollars a day that I know of."

"Bloomberg saves five hundred dollars a day?"

"Yeah, yeah!"

"How does he save five hundred dollars a day?"

"Every morning, when he goes to work, he goes in the subway," he explained. "You know in the subway, there is a five-hundred-dollar fine if you spit, so—he don't spit!"

LAURIE, JR.

## 106

One wash day, two women were doing a two-way broadcast of the local gossip, over the fence.

"Wasn't that something, the way Garfinkle's gas stove exploded last night?" gabbed one. "The explosion blew Mr. and Mrs. Garfinkle right out of the front door into the street!"

"Yeah," meowed the other, "that's the first time they've gone out together in thirty years!" FORD

## 107

I heard Orson Welles tell this story at the Players Club.

There was a cannibal tribe that couldn't get lend-lease, so they were slowly starving to death. One day, an actor on tour got lost and wandered into their midst and was quickly grabbed. In a jiffy, the cannibal chef rushed in to fix him all up, but the Chief stopped him.

"I know you are a big actor," said the Chief to the elected

one. "When I was with the World's Fair I saw you. You are a great comedian, a great tragedian, a great actor."

"Why we not cook him?" interrupted the impatient chef.

"You don't know actors," explained the Chief. "When you praise actors, they swell all up—puff all up. Now we all eat plenty!"                                     HERSHFIELD

### 108

By mistake, the notice of a gentleman's demise was inserted in the daily newspaper. The gentleman concerned was very much alive and very much concerned. He called the death-notice editor in a wrath.

"Say, listen, bud," he stormed, "did you put that notice of my death in the paper?"

The voice at the other end of the phone answered warily.

"Yes, I did," said the editor. "By the way—er—where are you calling from?"                                     FORD

### 109

A small worm was crawling along a road one day. The sun was very hot, and he stopped for a breather. Suddenly he noticed another worm come up next to him.

"Honey," said the first worm. "I could go for you. What say we two get married?"

"Don't be silly," answered the second. "I'm your other end."                                     HERSHFIELD

### 110

At a small boarding house on the outskirts of Washington lived a newly elected Senator. One day he flounced up to the landlady in a terrible dither.

"Madam," he stated flatly, "Madam, you must send a full-length mirror up to my room immediately!"

"But, Senator," said the woman, "you have a half-length mirror; isn't that all right? It's very pretty," she added wistfully.

"Madam, that will not do," said the Senator. "Three times, now, I have gone out without my pants on."     LAURIE, JR.

## 111

A henpecked husband I know will only go to a woman dentist. He says it makes him terribly happy to hear a dame tell him to open his mouth instead of shut it!     FORD

## 112

A woman went shopping in a crowded department store with her little boy, who had been listening to Red Skelton too often. They pushed into a packed elevator, and suddenly a big blonde standing in front of the kid turned around and clouted a much surprised man next to her, right across the mouth. She got off at the next floor in a huff.

"I wonder why she slapped that man?" said the mother to the little boy.

"I dunno," said the kid, "but she stepped on my little footie —and I pinched 'er."     LAURIE, JR.

## 113

A soldier came back to camp, after an attack, with a German helmet slung over his shoulder.

"I had to kill a hundred Germans for this," he announced.

"Why?" asked his buddies.

"Had to get the right size," he said.     FORD

**114**

An American, who was one of the last to leave Nazi Berlin, told me of an unusual experience he had there, just before he got out. This man went to a Berlin dentist and asked how much he would charge to pull a tooth. The dentist wanted one hundred dollars.

"Why, that's outrageous!" said the Yankee. "Back home my dentist would charge only ten dollars. Fifteen top. What's the big idea?"

"Over here it's different," said the dentist. "We pull it out through your ear. You can't open your mouth in Berlin!"

HERSHFIELD

**115**

A man bought one of those mail-order houses—the kind that comes in sections—and decided to save himself some money. He was going to put it together himself. After two months he had it all assembled, and invited all his friends over to see it.

"My goodness, Edmund," one friend exclaimed, "your house is upside down!"

"So that's it," said Edmund. "No wonder I keep falling off the porch!"                                FORD

**116**

Several inmates were sitting on the lawn in front of their nut house. It was a very hot midsummer afternoon and the boys were wilting. Finally one couldn't stand it any more. He went upstairs, took off his clothes, and filled the bathtub full of water. Then he climbed onto the washstand and did a fancy swan dive into the tub. He broke his nose. Again he climbed up on the washstand. Down he dived again and knocked out all his front teeth. The third time he cracked his head wide open.

"Oh," he said. "Low tide."                              LAURIE, JR.


## 117

A buck private in an army camp went strolling right past a young officer without saluting him.

"Hey, you!" yelled the officer after the retreating rookie, "come back here." He pointed to the bars on his shoulders. "Do you see this?"

"Are you complaining?" asked the rookie. "Look at the suit they gave me!"                              HERSHFIELD


## 118

A fancy woman hired a man to act as butler at an affair planned to put her on the upper crust. Everything had to be just so—Emily Post stuff.

"Now, Abercrombie," she said to the man, "I want you to announce all the people who arrive. You know the procedure, of course, Abercrombie?"

"Of course," said Abercrombie. In the interval before the guests arrived, Abercrombie decided to test the punch, and the more he tested, the better he liked it.

Suddenly the doorbell rang. Up to the door he rushed, and with as much composure as he could muster, ushered in Mr. and Mrs. Nichols with their three children.

"Mr. and Mrs. Nichols," announced Abercrombie, "and fifteen cents."                              FORD

**119**

A panhandler walked up to me in the street and grabbed me by the lapels. "Gimme a dime, mister," he said.

"What's the idea?" I said to him. "What's the idea of stopping people in the street asking for money?"

"What do you want me to do," said the panhandler, "open an office?" HERSHFIELD

**120**

Two men met in the street, and one had a terrible toothache. He was suffering. He was in agony. "What can I do to relieve this awful pain?" he moaned to his friend.

"You know what I do?" said the other guy helpfully. "When I have a toothache, or a pain, I go over to my wife, and she puts her arms around me, and caresses me, and soothes me until finally I forget all about the pain."

His friend brightened up immediately. "Gee, that's wonderful!" he exclaimed. "Is she home now?" LAURIE, JR.

**121**

A very stout woman and a very skinny one were both waiting for a trolley car. When it got to their corner the car was very crowded. The big fat gal pushed her way into the tram before the stringy one.

"It certainly is a shame they don't charge by the pound in these cars," said the skinny one cuttingly.

"If they did," her weighty companion answered, "if they did charge by the pound, they wouldn't stop for you at all." FORD

**122**

Three men went fishing in a small rowboat, and suddenly found themselves in a heavy squall. The boat sprang a leak and sank, and they all found themselves in the water. Two of the men began to swim, but the third floundered and sputtered helplessly. He was sinking.

"Say, Harold," one of the swimmers asked him, "can you float alone?"

"Look!" said the floundering one. "I'm drowning and he talks business!" HERSHFIELD

**123**

"What a lovely gift," said the salesman. "Why won't you buy this lovely gift? Your wife would love it!"

"I have two wives," said the customer.

"What?" said the salesman aghast. "Are you a bigamist?"

"No," said the man, "but my daughter just got married." FORD

**124**

A man in a restaurant called the waiter over disgustedly.

"What do you call this stuff—coffee or tea?" he sneered. "It tastes like kerosene!"

"If it tastes like kerosene," said the waiter calmly, "it must be coffee. The tea tastes like turpentine." HERSHFIELD

**125**

A wise little kid said to his teacher: "A woman got on the bus with a sixteen-year-old daughter, and had to pay full fare —ten cents. Another woman got on with her six-year-old child and had to pay half-fare—five cents. A little later, a woman got on with no children at all and she didn't have to pay any fare."

"Why not?" she asked.

"Because she had a transfer!" informed her pupil.

LAURIE, JR.

## 126

A little boy's father died from overindulgence in liquor. After the funeral, the little boy said to his mother, "Mama! When I go to Heaven, how will I know Papa?"

"Just look for an angel with a red nose," she suggested.

FORD

## 127

It was midnight in the jungle! The ping of Jap snipers could be heard interspersed with shrill hair-raising cries of wild animals! Clancy and Finnegan were on a dangerous scouting mission. Beads of perspiration popped on Clancy's fevered brow! "Are you nervous?" whispered Finnegan hoarsely.

"Not a bit!" assured the trembling Clancy, weakly.

"Then why are you wiping my face?" asked Finnegan.

HERSHFIELD

## 128

A fellow went into a little second-hand clothing store carrying a suit. He addressed the proprietor: "I want my money back," he demanded. "The pockets of this suit are full of moths!"

"Now don't get excited," pleaded the proprietor. "How much did you pay for the suit?"

"Seven bucks!"

"Seven bucks and you found moths?" declared the proprietor. "What do you want in your pockets for seven dollars—humming birds?"                    LAURIE, JR.

## 129

Two fellows, who hadn't seen each other in years met. "What are you doing now?" asked one.

"I'm a panhandler," replied the other.

"Panhandler?" remarked the other in surprise. "You mean —a beggar?"

"No," he explained. "I run a beauty parlor—I handle pans!"                                              FORD

## 130

An American prisoner in Germany raised an awful rumpus, condemning the heads of the whole Nazi regime. He was loud and vociferous.

"Hitler smells! Goering smells! Goebbels smells!" he shouted at the top of his voice.

There was no stopping him, so he was taken before the high military court over which Goering presided.

"Hitler smells! Goering smells! Goebbels smells!" the American prisoner kept shouting.

Unable to control himself, Goebbels approached him threateningly.

"You fresh American!" he hissed. "You're asking for it and you'll get it! Frank Sinatra smells!"        HERSHFIELD

**131**

Mrs. Feigelbaum went into Rappaport's millinery store and tried on every hat in the place. All she did was put them on and take them off! As Rappaport watched her he became more and more burned up. Finally she came over to him.

"Mr. Rappaport, I've tried on every hat in the place and nothing is becoming to me," she complained. "Have you got any more?"

"Listen, Mrs. Feigelbaum," he replied coldly, "today, we're selling hats—not faces!"                    LAURIE, JR.

**132**

A Wolf in an auto spotted a cute little blonde on the corner waiting for a bus. He jammed on his brakes, pouring on the personality. "Hello, sweetheart!" he called, "do you want a ride?"

"Which direction are you going?" she asked, building him up.

"North!" he informed, hopefully.

"Fine!" she exclaimed. "Give my regards to the Eskimos!"                    FORD

**133**

Three morons entered a country drugstore. "I'd like ten cents' worth of that peppermint candy you have on that top shelf," said the first, indicating.

The proprietor nodded, went to the corner of the store, took a ladder, brought it back, climbed up to the top shelf, filled a bag with candy, climbed down, replaced the ladder in the corner and handed him the bag.

"I'd like ten cents' worth of that peppermint candy, too!" informed the second moron. So, the proprietor had to go through the same tedious routine again to get him a bag of candy; but when he was at the top of the ladder he hesitated before coming down and looked at the third moron.

"Do you want ten cents' worth of this candy, too?" he inquired.

"No," the third one replied.

The proprietor climbed down, gave the second moron his bag of candy and replaced the ladder in the corner.

"What do you want?" he asked the third moron.

"I want five cents' worth of that candy!" he replied.

HERSHFIELD

## 134

A fellow went into a millinery store. "I'd like to buy a big Satan hat for my wife," he informed.

"You mean satin," corrected the saleslady. "Satan is something that looks like the devil!"

"Did you ever see my wife?" inquired the fellow.

LAURIE, JR.

## 135

Mr. and Mrs. Wonkle saved all of their gas coupons, then drove to Yellowstone Park. As they approached their destination, Mrs. Wonkle peered through the windshield.

"Look," she exclaimed gleefully, "there's Old Faithful, the geyser!"

"That's no geyser," informed Mr. Wonkle, "that's our radiator boiling over!"

FORD

**136**

When he got into the Army, little Sammy was advised to act tough. "That's the only way to get along and command respect," warned his friend. So Sammy carried out his advice to a "T" and swaggered all around the camp acting loud and talking out of the corner of his mouth. Repeatedly warned to pipe down, Sammy ignored the tip that he would get in trouble if he didn't.

"Show me a Sergeant, and I'll show you a dope!" shouted Sammy, loudly. The words were no sooner spoken when a big six-foot Sergeant appeared. He looked down at little Sammy pugnaciously.

"I'm a Sergeant!" he bellowed.

"I'm a dope!" whispered Sammy.                    HERSHFIELD

**137**

One day last summer, a long line of people were waiting in front of a ticket-office window in the Grand Central Depot. A young woman crowded in at the head of the line which aroused the anger of those who had been patiently waiting for some time.

"Mister!" she called to the ticket seller. "Where can I go for five dollars?"

Before he could answer, the whole line of people told her!
                    LAURIE, JR.

**138**

In court, a Judge took up the questioning of a defendant. "I understand that your wife is scared to death of you?" he said.

"That's right, your Honor," admitted the defendant. The Judge leaned over and whispered in his ear. "As man to man," he said, "how do you do it?"    FORD

## 139

Mrs. Bacigaloupe went into Tony's General Store and purchased various things including—spaghetti. When she returned home, she began to cook the spaghetti, then stopped and phoned Tony's. "This is Mrs. Bacigaloupe," she said, "you gotta be more careful, Tony—I found a shoelace in the spaghetti!"

"I'm-a glad you tell-a me!" exclaimed Tony. "You owe-a me twelve more points!"    HERSHFIELD

## 140

"Gee, my sister's lucky at parties," boasted a little kid. "Why?" asked the other kid.

"She went to a big party the other night," explained the first one, "and they played kissing games. The men were blindfolded and had to run around the room and catch a girl. Then they take the blindfold off and if the fellow didn't kiss her, he'd have to give her a pound of candy. Is my sister lucky!"

"What do you mean—lucky?"

"She came back home with fifteen pounds of candy!"

LAURIE, JR.

## 141

A Marine returned from Australia after doing a swell job in the Solomons. He was invited to a party and met a stunning looking girl who immediately engaged him in conversation about his experiences with the Japs.

"The first day I was in action," he said, "I killed two Japs with my bare hands!"

"Which hand did you kill them with?" asked the stunner in wide-eyed admiration.

"I killed one with my right hand," he said, "and one with my left hand!"

Overcome with emotion, she kissed his right hand first, and then his left one.

Another Leatherneck standing by watching the proceedings addressed the girl. "Listen, Beautiful," he cracked, "this guy told you how he killed a Jap with each hand and you kissed them both. I'm here to tell you that I killed one hundred Japs and I bit them all to death!"                    FORD

## 142

Sammy Ginsberg went into a Nazi saloon in Berlin. "I want a whiskey and soda!" he demanded.

"You've got a lot of nerve coming in here, Ginsberg!" replied the bartender. "Get out quick—before something happens to you!"

Reluctantly, Sammy took his advice and left. A minute after, an Allied plane flew over the saloon and dropped a bomb on it, leaving it a shambles! The bartender was extricating himself from the debris when Sammy returned.

"Do I get the whiskey and soda?" asked Sammy, threateningly, "or do I have to do it all over again!"

HERSHFIELD

## 143

As she came out of the subway, Sadie Rappaport encountered a friend. "I just met Mr. and Mrs. Bloomberg in the subway," gushed Sadie. "Is he a wonderful man! Is he courtesy!"

"What do you mean 'is he courtesy'!" asked her friend, puzzled.

"Well, Mr. Bloomberg saw that I was very tired from the whole day's work—all pipped out," explained Sadie, "so he made his wife get up and give me her seat!"    LAURIE, JR.

## 144

Dopey Dilldock was looking rather crestfallen when Ditsey Baumwortle ran into him. "What's the matter, Dopey?" asked Ditsey. "You look very sad, indeed—any trouble?"

"I am rather sad, indeed," declared Dopey, "because last week I saw a fellow hit a girl!"

"Did you let him get away with it?" inquired Ditsey.

"I did not!" assured Dopey. "I walked right over to him and said, 'Look here, my friend, don't you know you're a coward when you strike a lady? Why don't you try hitting a man?' I just came out of the hospital this morning!" he concluded.    FORD

## 145

A pale, sickly, and very seedy looking book salesman made repeated efforts to see the head of a big concern, without success. One day, he managed to trap him as he was entering his office. "I want you to take an order for a book I'm selling," he said.

"What's the name of it?" snapped the boss.

"*Health, Wealth and Happiness*," informed the salesman.

The boss gave him a quick appraising glance. "I'll buy it," he promised, "on the condition that you read it."

"No use," moaned the salesman. "I wrote it!"

HERSHFIELD

## 146

After taking a handful of soot from the chimney and throwing it all over the living-room rug, then grabbing a handful of ashes and scattering them all over the floor and tearing up a newspaper into little bits and flinging them around, a salesman who was demonstrating vacuum cleaners turned to the lady of the house who was watching him in silence. "You're going to be surprised how quickly I clean this up!" he said. "Now tell me, where's the plug so I can put this socket in?"

"You're going to be surprised," remarked the lady. "We have no electricity!"

LAURIE, JR.

## 147

George Trommer told Sherman Billingsley and me this story one night at the Stork Club.

Dugan got a job as head of the sales department for a lumber company. One day, his boss phoned him to test his astuteness.

"I want to order a thousand knot-holes," exclaimed the boss.

"Now ain't that a shame," answered Dugan. "I just sold the last thousand knot-holes to a brewery!"

"What would a brewery be doing with a thousand knot-holes?" inquired the boss.

"They use knot-holes for bungholes in the barrels!" informed Dugan.

FORD

**148**

During rationing period in New York, a fellow tried to sell a Dictionary to one of the heads of the Department of Agriculture.

"It's modern and up-to-date," assured the salesman; "in fact, it's right off the press."

"I'll take a peek at it," consented the prospective buyer. He looked up the word "cow"—it said—"see bovine." He turned to the word "bovine" and it said—"see beef." He looked up "beef" and it said—"see La Guardia"!

HERSHFIELD

**149**

Mrs. Ginnis and Mrs. Doyle met downtown and stopped to converse.

"I just left Mrs. Casey," gushed Mrs. Ginnis. "You know, she's a very wealthy woman now—she won the Sweepstakes!"

"I read that in the paper," remarked Mrs. Doyle.

"She's got a limousine this year!" continued Mrs. Ginnis.

"Last year she had a carbuncle!" snapped Mrs. Doyle, unimpressed.          LAURIE, JR.

**150**

One oaf was driving a car cross-country while the other oaf studied a road map.

"Stop the car!" suddenly commanded the oaf with the map.

"Why?" asked the driver, in surprise.

"It says here to follow the street car," said the oaf indicating the map, "and we've got to wait until one comes along!"          FORD

**151**

Mrs. Pinkus went to the theater to see Al Jolson. She sat in the front row. Whenever Jolson appeared, she said, "Ah, good! Ah, good!" which Al could not help hearing and which pleased him no end. After the show, he hastened out of his dressing room and waited to see her.

"My name's Jolson," he said. "I want to thank you for being such an appreciative audience."

"What?" replied the surprised Mrs. Pinkus.

"All through the show you were saying 'Ah, good! Ah, good!' and I heard you."

"I've got rheumatism," she explained, "and when they put that very strong light on you, it hit my back, and oh, boy— was that good!" HERSHFIELD

**152**

Bloomberg had a little hotel in the Catskills. To secure entertainment, he came to New York. Among others, he interviewed a mimic.

"I give imitations of people," explained the mimic.

"For instance?" inquired Bloomberg.

"I'll give you an imitation of President Roosevelt." He did so.

"Very good," complimented Bloomberg. "Now make for me Churchill." He gave a perfect imitation of him.

"You're all right," complimented Bloomberg again.

A deal was closed for one hundred dollars a week. At the end of the week, business was off, so Bloomberg paid the mimic ten dollars.

"What's this?" asked the mimic, puzzled.

"Business is bad," explained Bloomberg.

"Ten dollars is no good to me," protested the mimic. "I have to pay for my apartment in New York, pay my wife alimony, and pay for food and clothing. Give me some dough—I need it!"

"You're a mimic?" reminded Bloomberg. "Then make like Rockefeller!"                                    LAURIE, JR.

## 153

Dugan and Hogan, a couple of laborers, stopped in front of Tiffany's window to look at a tray of sparkling diamonds. "How would you like to have your pick?" asked Dugan.

"I'd rather have my shovel," replied Hogan. "I could get more!"                                                    FORD

## 154

A woman, testifying for alimony, described her plight. "I'm going around with practically not a stitch of clothes on, your Honor," she declared, "while my husband buys jewelry for chorus girls! He gave one of them a diamond ring. He gave another a diamond bracelet! He's a regular gigolo!"

"Let's get this straight," summarized the Judge. "When women give him jewelry—he's a gigolo. When he gives it to them—he's a sucker!"                              HERSHFIELD

## 155

A fellow told a friend how he returned home unexpectedly and caught his wife kissing a man.

"Why didn't you shoot him!" asked the indignant friend.

"What, shoot a guy every week?" replied the knowing husband.                                              LAURIE, JR.

**156**

Mrs. Snapgirdle was a very extravagant woman and her husband was a very stingy little weasel. "I wonder what women will wear in Heaven?" she remarked.

"I suppose you'd want to buy the most expensive clothes," he snapped, "the same as you do on earth!"

"That's something you won't have to worry about," she assured, "you won't be up there to pay for them!"

FORD

**157**

Three nosy women were seated on the veranda at a Summer Resort, "putting it on" about their respective husbands.

"Your husband's a lawyer, isn't he?" asked one.

"No," replied the other, "he's a Barrister."

She turned to the other woman.

"Your husband's a writer, isn't he?" she inquired.

"A Scenario Writer," corrected the other woman, then asked, "Isn't your husband a waiter?"

"No, he's not a waiter," replied the woman, "he's the contact man between the customers and the Chef!"

HERSHFIELD

**158**

A little boy was sent to the grocery store for a half-pound of honey. En route, he stopped to play around a while with the result that when he got to the store, he forgot what he was sent for. The grocer tried to help him out, guessing everything possible, but to no avail. At this point, he called his three-hundred-pound wife.

"Honey! Come here and see if you can guess what this little boy wants!"

"That's it!" beamed the kid, "I want a half pound of her!"

LAURIE, JR.

## 159

"Papa, there's a limerick contest in the newspaper," said a little kid to his father. "I can win a hundred dollars if I guess the last words. Will you help me out?"

"Get your mother to do it," suggested his father. "She's better at last words than I am!"

FORD

## 160

Realizing she had to reduce, a very hefty girl went to see a doctor.

"You'll never reduce at home," he warned, "temptations are too great. You'll have to join a health club and reduce systematically."

She took his advice and joined a health club, religiously following the rigid diet and long walks. Each morning, she would lift the window shade in her bedroom to see how the weather was and dress accordingly. On the fifteenth day, she lifted the window shade and—went up with it!

HERSHFIELD

## 161

At the New York Press Club, Roy Howard, of Scripps-Howard, panicked us all with this one.

"My name's Goldberg," announced a man to the newspaper editor.

"What about it?" inquired the editor.

"You've got it in your paper today that I'm dead," declared Goldberg.

"There must be some mistake," assured the editor, "and we're very sorry."

"Very sorry," sneered Goldberg, contemptuously. "Do you realize what a fix I'd be in today if I was one of those guys that believe everything I read in the paper?"

LAURIE, JR.

## 162

A grocer passed away. He rapped on the gates of Hades asking permission to enter.

"What do you want to come in here for?" inquired Satan.

"I want to collect some bills from some of my customers who died before I did," informed the grocer.

"What makes you think your customers are here?" asked Satan.

"Because every time I tried to collect from them," explained the grocer, "this is where they told me to go!"

FORD

## 163

The proprietor of a Catskill Mountain Summer Resort got word that the son of one of his guests, Mrs. Pinkus, was a newspaper reporter. With an eye on free publicity, he immediately gave her the best room with Southern exposure, the best food, and when it came to pay her room rent, presented her with a due-bill.

"That's very nice of you to treat me like this," declared Mrs. Pinkus. "I greatly appreciate it."

"By the way," remarked the proprietor, "I hear your son is a newspaper reporter."

"Yes," she replied, "he reports how many newspapers are left on the stand every night."                    HERSHFIELD

## 164

Mrs. Bloomberg entered her husband's office unannounced and unexpectedly and found his secretary sitting on his lap. "Don't get excited," warned Mr. Bloomberg, sensing trouble, "I didn't want to tell you that business is so bad, I'm studying how to become a ventriloquist!"                    LAURIE, JR.

## 165

Little Tommy was being instructed in courtesy by his mother. "If you happen to be riding in a crowded streetcar and an older person comes in," she said, "always get up and give them your seat."

Tommy nodded in understanding.

A few days later, he was seated on his mother's lap in a crowded streetcar when a man entered. Tommy quickly got off his mother's lap.

"Will you have my seat, sir?" he asked politely.    FORD

## 166

The last time I was in Chicago I was seated next to John Hertz, head of the Yellow Cab Company, at a banquet in his honor at the Chicago Athletic Club, and he told this story.

A moron from the country arrived at a New York City depot. He hailed a taxicab.

"The Acme Hotel," he said, not realizing it was directly across the street. The wise taxi driver didn't say a word but drove him down Riverside Drive, then to Yonkers, to Canarsie and Brooklyn. He finally returned and dropped the moron off in front of the Acme Hotel.

"Ten dollars!" he said, holding out his hand.

"Oh, no, you don't!" hollered the moron. "You ain't got no sucker in me! The last time I was here I came out of the same station and went to this same hotel and the driver only charged me five dollars!"                                        HERSHFIELD

## 167

A Scotchman who lived in New York bought a homing pigeon. His sweetheart lived in Philadelphia, so the Scotchman figured he'd save money by sending messages to her with the pigeon. For some time his scheme worked out fine, but one day the pigeon failed to return. While worrying about it, the doorbell rang and the Scotchman opened the door. A taxi driver was standing there holding the pigeon and a small slip of paper.

"Do you own this pigeon?" asked the driver.

"Yes, that's my pigeon!" declared the Scotchman, joyfully.

"Well, you owe me thirty-three dollars and sixty cents!" he said, indicating the slip.

"What's the idea?" asked the Scotchman, stunned.

"On the way back," explained the pigeon, "it looked like rain, so I thought I'd take a cab!"                                LAURIE, JR.

## 168

Two dopes went to the Menagerie and came to the Ostrich cage. "You know," informed one, "that's the biggest living bird?"

"It ain't only the biggest living bird," replied the other, "it's the biggest bird when it's dead, too!"     FORD

## 169

A moron went to the Board of Health to enter a complaint. "I've got six brothers and we all live in one room," he reported. "My brothers have pets in the room, too. One has twelve monkeys and another has twelve dogs. There's no air in the room and it's terrible! You've got to do something about it!"

"Have you got windows?" asked the man who was recording the complaint.

"Yeah," answered the moron.

"Why don't you open them?" he suggested.

"What?" hollered the moron in shocked indignation, "and lose all my pigeons?"     HERSHFIELD

## 170

Lazy Zeke was sitting in a rocker on his front porch in the Ozarks, smoking. "I just noticed somethin', Zeke," drawled his neighbor, "you've got your left shoe on your right foot and your right shoe on your left foot."

"What do you think of that?" drawled the surprised Zeke. "For the past twenty years I thought I had a club foot!"

     LAURIE, JR.

## 171

Up in my home town, there's a funny little newspaper that's so full of ads there's hardly room for news. A couple of weeks ago, the editor ran a little box on the front page that read—"Due to the lack of space, we are not running some of the news. Consequently, the birth of nine babies will have to be postponed until next week!"     FORD

## 172

Mrs. Pinkus had supper waiting, but her husband, little Pinkus, didn't come home. About nine o'clock, he phoned her. "I'll tell you what happened," he said. "I was walking home minding my own business, when a big tough teamster, about three hundred pounds, started to insult me. So, I said, 'Come on, you big bum, I don't care for your size—come off the truck and fight like a man!' While he was getting down from his truck, I took off my coat, rolled up my sleeves and then—did he beat the life out of me!"

HERSHFIELD

## 173

An excitable woman dashed into Wanamaker's and raced to the girdle department.

"You know that girdle I got yesterday?" she said to the floorlady. "Well, it's all wrong—it isn't for me!"

"Just a minute," replied the floorlady. "Didn't we make it to order for you?"

"Yes," agreed the nervous one, "but it isn't for me—it isn't for me!"

"Why not?" inquired the floorlady, puzzled.

"When I brought it home and unwrapped it," said the fluttery one, "I looked on the box and it said 'Made especially for John Wanamaker'!—it isn't for me!"     LAURIE, JR.

## 174

A farmer who had never been away from home, suddenly decided to go on a sight-seeing trip of the United States.

Seated opposite him in the train arriving in Chicago was one of those very ultra society dames with an eyeglass on a stick! Before arriving at the depot, the train stopped briefly at the Stock Yards. She quickly extracted a bottle of smelling salts from her bag and removed the cork to overcome the Eau de Stock Yards stench. After a couple of whiffs the farmer became annoyed.

"Lady, would you mind putting the cork back in that bottle?" he requested. "Whatever you've got in there is smelling up the whole car!"                                    FORD

## 175

The first official sight-seeing trip in America was made by Daniel Boone, which reminds me of the historian who read that when Daniel Boone traveled through the wilderness he carved on a certain tree the following words—"I am the first white person to ever travel through this wilderness." The historian decided to find the tree to see if what he had read was fact or fiction. After hunting through the wilderness for weeks, he discovered the tree, but underneath Boone's carved declaration was—"That's what you think.—Eleanor Roosevelt!"                                    HERSHFIELD

## 176

A screwball went into a New York Gin Mill. "Give me two glasses of whiskey for me and my friend," he said.

"Where's your friend?" asked the bartender.

"He's away out in California," replied the screwball. So, the bartender gave him one glass of whiskey.

"I want two glasses of whiskey," insisted the crackpot, "for me and my friend!"

"I can't give your friend a glass of whiskey," said the bartender. "He's away out in California."

"I was just kidding," declared the screwball. "He's only in Cleveland!" LAURIE, JR.

## 177

Mrs. Snedeker went to the grocery store to buy some eggs. When the clerk told her they were sixty cents a dozen, she protested. "Sixty cents a dozen," she exclaimed indignantly, "why that's five cents a piece for an egg!"

"Correct," replied the clerk, "but you must remember that one egg represents a whole day's work for a hen!" FORD

## 178

A very homely looking woman walked into a department store. "I want thirty-two feet of veiling for my hat!" she said.

"You mean two feet," replied the saleslady.

"No, thirty-two feet," insisted the ugly duckling. "My husband's gotten to a point where he has more fun hunting for my face than finding it!" HERSHFIELD

## 179

Bloomberg and Epstein met. "Weinstein invited me to visit him for a couple of weeks in the Catskills," informed Bloomberg.

"Did you accept his invitation?" inquired Epstein.

"I went, but I had a funny experience," reminisced Bloomberg. "I got a bus to the Catskills and when it arrived, I found out I was in Baltimore!"

"What did you do?"

"I went back to New York and took a bus to the Catskills again and arrived safe and sound—in Baltimore!"

"What did you do then?"

"I went back to New York and took a bus for Baltimore and arrived safe and sound—in the Catskills!"          LAURIE, JR.

## 180

A very stout woman, built like a cross-wise blimp, took a train to visit her mother. Hours later, she complained to the conductor.

"Mister Conductor," she protested, "I'm so stout that I have to get off backwards, and every time I try to get off the porter thinks I'm trying to get on, and shoves me back in again. I'm five stations past where I want to go now!"

FORD

## 181

A distracted fellow dashed into the police station at three o'clock in the morning.

"Captain, you've got to help me!" he pleaded. "My wife's out every night gambling! She's a fiend for it—neglects the children and her home and I have to get my own supper. It's terrible! Now, at three o'clock in the morning she's still away from home—gambling!"

"Do you know where?" asked the Police Captain.

"Yes. She's playing Gin Rummy in a clubroom on the corner of Grand Boulevard!"

"Tell you what I'll do," suggested the obliging Captain. "I'll throw the fear of God into her. I'll send a police car and raid the place!"

"That's fine," enthused the man; then after a brief moment added, "but Captain, do you think you can arrange it without arresting my mother?"                    HERSHFIELD

## 182

The proud mother of a little boy was bragging about her offspring to a friend.

"He's really smart," beamed the mother. "Some day soon, he'll be a Quiz kid!"

Just then the kid entered. "Hey, Mama," he called, "is Daddy a dog?"

"No, my dear," she replied, somewhat embarrassed, "where did you ever get an idea like that?"

"Well," mused the kid, "I just heard the cook tell the iceman that she was going to tie a can to Daddy!"

                                                    LAURIE, JR.

## 183

A well-known stockbroker, who was a habitué of night clubs, suddenly went broke. A friend of his met him months later.

"I never see you in the night clubs any more," he remarked.

"It used to be Wine, Women, and Song," explained the financially flattened one, "but now it's Beer, Mama, and the Radio!"                                        FORD

## 184

A fourteen-dollar-a-week clerk was driving an auto, running around spending in night clubs and dressing in the height of fashion. His boss became suspicious and called him into his private office.

"Where do you get all of the money to do those things?" he demanded.

"Every Saturday I hold a raffle," explained the clerk. "I sell thousands of tickets at a quarter each."

"What do you raffle?" inquired the boss.

"My salary!" replied the clerk.                    HERSHFIELD

## 185

Two Italians met.

"Hey, Tony," inquired one, "is-a your boy working?"

"Sure," replied Tony, "he's-a working very hard, making a lotta money. He's-a work sixteen-a hours a day!"

"Is-a he a Union man?" asked his friend.

"Sure, he's-a Union man!"

"And works sixteen-a hours a day?" questioned the friend. "Don't you know the Union only allows a man to work-a eight-a hours a day?"

"I know," assured Tony, "but he belongs-a to two Unions!"

LAURIE, JR.

## 186

A man entered the living room of his home and discovered a dopey guy proposing to his daughter.

"Hey, listen you!" shouted the irate father threateningly. "I'll teach you to make love to my daughters!"

"I wish you would," replied the dopey one. "I'm not making much headway!"                    FORD

## 187

A moron was sitting on a wall near a railroad track with eyes glued on the tunnel. A fellow appeared and stopped.

"What are you doing here?" he asked.

"I'm watching the trains going into the tunnel," replied the moron. "There must be some beautiful girl in there!"

"What makes you think there must be some beautiful girl in the tunnel?" asked the man, puzzled.

"Because," explained the moron, "when the trains go in they go—'A-whoo!'—and when they come out they go—'Ha-Ha-Ha-Ha'! " HERSHFIELD

## 188

Bloomberg was laughing hysterically. "What are you laughing about?" inquired his pal, Moe.

"I'll tell you," said Bloomberg, hardly able to control himself. "Two weeks ago, I knocked off work early—instead of leaving at six o'clock I went home at five o'clock, and did I get a surprise!"

"What was the surprise?" asked Moe.

"I found my foreman sitting on the couch in my house kissing my wife!"

"What did you do?" inquired Moe.

"Nothing," said Bloomberg, with a shrug, "but last week I went home an hour earlier as a surprise and saw the foreman on the couch kissing my wife again!"

"What did you do?" asked Moe. "Hit him?"

"Hit him?" echoed Bloomberg in surprise. "No, I sold the couch!" LAURIE, JR.

## 189

A man was haled into court for pilfering fruit from a corner fruit stand. The Judge fined him ten dollars for impersonating a policeman! FORD

**190**

A Garden Party for Charity featured games of chance. Two morons were among the guests.

"I took a five-dollar chance for charity," said one, "and a big blonde gave me a kiss for buying it!" He peered cautiously around, then added, "I hate to say it, but she kisses better than my wife!"

The other moron immediately extracted a five-dollar bill from his wallet, left, and in a short time reappeared.

"Did she kiss good?" inquired the first moron.

"Swell," admitted the other, "but not better than your wife!"                    HERSHFIELD

**191**

A few years ago, millions of wild monkeys infested Japan and began destroying the gardens. It became so serious, the Japanese Big Shots held a meeting and decided to import baboons to kill the monkeys—which they did. The baboons killed the monkeys but there were so many they overran the place—so that problem had to be solved, too. The Japanese Big Shots held another meeting.

"Too many baboons," declared the spokesman. "Soon all Japan full of baboons! Tomorrow every Japanese take a club and as soon as they see baboon—hit him over the head! But, we all must have buttons on so we don't kill each other!"

                    LAURIE, JR.

**192**

Two Scotchmen, Sandy and MacPherson, were traveling on a train. As Sandy pulled out his handkerchief, a full set of false teeth fell to the floor! "Sandy," remarked MacPherson, "I wasn't aware that you had false teeth!"

"I haven't a false tooth in my head," replied Sandy. "They're my wife's. You see, she developed the pernicious and extravagant habit of eating between meals and I'm taking this precaution of stopping it!" FORD

### 193

Two soldiers, Mose and Rastus, were in a fox hole in Guadalcanal. For weeks, they had been in the thickest of the fray, fighting through rain and sleet, and going without food for days! During a lull in the battle, each received a letter from home. "Dat old gal of mine done wrote me she just married a pal of mine," informed Rastus.

"Ah got a letter from de Draft Board," confided Mose. "It says ah am to report fo' mah physical!" HERSHFIELD

### 194

One evening, a fellow brought home a guest for dinner. "Is our dinner ready?" asked the husband.

"Did you bring it?" asked the wife.

"Bring what?" replied her puzzled husband.

"You told me over the phone you were bringing home a squab for dinner," she said.

"I didn't say squab," corrected the husband. "I said I was bringing home a slob!" LAURIE, JR.

### 195

When I attended a party of Governor Earl Warren's in San Francisco, he told this story.

A Floridian went to California. As he walked around a garden, he picked up a watermelon. "Are these the biggest cucumbers you raise?" asked the Floridian.

"Put down that raisin!" advised the Californian.    FORD

## 196

A colored fellow had courted Mandy for nine years, but he was too bashful and shy to propose to her. One day he summoned enough courage to pop the vital question to her over the phone.

"Mandy," he began, "ah got a house, ah got an automobile and ah got money in de bank. Will you-all marry me?"

"Sure nuff, honey child!" replied Mandy, "but who-all is dis speaking?"    HERSHFIELD

## 197

Two fellows met.

"Are you keeping company?" asked one.

"Sure, with Sadie Glutz," informed the other. "She's a little-bitty kid—weighs ninety pounds. She's a regular pin-up girl. Are you keeping company?"

"Yes, with Sarah Bilge," replied the other. "She weighs three hundred pounds. She's a regular 'oomph' girl."

"What do you mean, an 'oomph' girl?" asked the first fellow.

"Every time she sits on the sofa," explained the other, "the sofa goes—'oomph'!"    LAURIE, JR.

## 198

A pessimist entered a restaurant and looked over the menu. "You have two steaks here," he said to the waitress, "one is a dollar and one is a dollar and a quarter. What's the difference between the two?"

"With the dollar-and-a-quarter steak you get a knife," she advised, "and with the dollar steak you get a harness!"

FORD

## 199

An Irish couple and an English couple got together and went to a Summer Resort to spend their vacation. They were most affable. In the afternoon, while the men played cards, the women would go fishing, for both of their husbands were very fond of fish. One day, Mrs. Clancy got a nibble on her line. After great difficulty, she brought in her catch—a great big eel! The Englishwoman enthused. "I say, Mrs. Clancy, you have an eel for your husband."

"Yes!" snapped Mrs. Clancy, "and you've got a jerk for yours!"

HERSHFIELD

## 200

One night Mr. and Mrs. Bloomberg were walking home from a party. No word had been spoken since they left.

"What are you mad at me about?" inquired Bloomberg.

"You disgraced me tonight!" she replied.

"What? How? When?" asked her surprised husband.

"When Mrs. Epstein was at the table, she said, 'Mr. Bloomberg, please pass your plate,' and you took out your teeth and said—'upper or lower?' "

LAURIE, JR.

## 201

Ditsey Baumwortle and Ockie Bopp were discussing their "Theory of Relativity."

"My Uncle Decatur must be nuts!" declared Ditsey. "In zero weather like this, he joins a nudist colony!"

"He must be fooling you," remarked Ockie, "because I saw your Uncle Decatur last night and he had on a blue suit!"

"That was no blue suit," informed Ditsey, "that was my Uncle Decatur!"                                         FORD

## 202

A big, goofy hillbilly was in the Army, but acted very disconsolate.

"What's the matter with you?" asked a soldier. "Don't you like Army life?"

"No," confessed the hillbilly.

"We all have to go through some discomfort," reminded the soldier. "After all, it's a war. Maybe you don't like getting up early in the morning—or the food?"

"I get enough sleep and the food is great," replied the hillbilly.

"Something about the Army is upsetting you, isn't it?"

"Yes," admitted the hillbilly, "the bullets—they're real!"
                                                    HERSHFIELD

## 203

A woman sent a letter to the editor of "Advice to Lovelorn." She wrote—"Dear Editor: I'm a very young woman married to a very old man. My husband's best friend is a handsome young man who is in love with me. What should I do?"

The editor answered on the back of the letter—"My dear Madam: It isn't right for you to think of the handsome young man. The only decent thing you can do is to put poison in your husband's coffee!"    LAURIE, JR.

## 204

Mr. Printwhistle was away from his home town for over a year. When he returned he met an old friend.

"Are you and Sadie married?" asked the friend.

"No," confessed Printwhistle, "the whole year I was away, I wrote her a letter of proposal every day. She saw so much of the postman, that she married him!"    FORD

## 205

Little Private Sammy was on guard duty at headquarters. "I'm expecting General Eisenhower," informed the Lieutenant. "Let me know the minute he arrives!"

They saluted and the Lieutenant departed. Soon after he returned.

"Did he arrive yet?" inquired the Lieutenant.

"No," said Sammy, and saluted.

"Let me know the minute General Eisenhower arrives. It's very important!"

Again they saluted and the Lieutenant left, then returned again asking the same question.

Finally General Eisenhower arrived.

"Pardon me," challenged Sammy, "are you General Eisenhower?"

"Yes," replied the General.

"Oh," wailed Sammy, "are you going to get it from the Lieutenant!"    HERSHFIELD

## 206

"How's that big bum brother of yours?" inquired a fellow. "Is he still out of work?"

"He's doing marvelous," informed the other brother. "He's driving around in a swell big car all day with a pocket full of dough!"

"What's he doing?" asked the fellow.

"He's a conductor on a bus!" replied the bum's brother.

LAURIE, JR.

**207**

Just before the last Presidential election, one of those modern, New Deal women left a political meeting, came home, threw her hat on the table, slumped down on the divan, lit a cigarette and made a prediction to her henpecked husband.

"Homer," she said, "we're going to sweep the country!"

"Well," suggested Homer, timidly, "if you're going to sweep the country, I wish you'd start with the living room!"

FORD

**208**

A wounded colored soldier was brought to the base hospital. The interne asked him how he got shot up so badly.

"Ah was startin' to charge when some snipers shot me in mah left leg," he explained. "Ah got up and dey shot me in mah right arm. Ah got up and dey shot me in mah left arm. Ah went down again!"

"Then what happened?" inquired the interested interne.

"Ah figured it was 'bout time ah told dem somethin', so ah hollered 'Shoot at somebody else—ah'm not de whole Army!' "

HERSHFIELD

**209**

This is Winston Churchill's favorite story. When the Nazis were bombing London, a housewife was cleaning up her home. Her husband, who was in the bomb shelter, called to her.

"Come on down here in the cellar, where it's safe!"

"Not until I finish," she replied.

"What are you cleaning up for?" he asked.

"In case they blow out the front door," she explained, "I want everything to look neat!"                                              LAURIE, JR.

## 210

When the noontime whistle blew, Dugan limped out for lunch.

"What are you limping for?" asked his foreman. "Have you got a sore foot?"

"I have a nail in my shoe," groaned Dugan.

"Why don't you take it out?" inquired the foreman.

"What?" replied Dugan, indignantly. "In me lunch hour?"

                                                                FORD

## 211

A father took his little son Milton to the Zoo.

"See, Milton," he said, "those are wild animals. If they ever got out of those cages, they'd tear a person to pieces!"

"Poppa, if that lion should come out and grab a hold of you and tear you to pieces," said Milton, "what number bus do I take to get home?"                                     HERSHFIELD

## 212

"Listen, Darling," protested a henpecked husband. "Why don't you stop picking on me? I'm trying to do everything possible to make you happy!"

"You don't do one thing my first husband did to make me happy!" she argued.

"What's that?" inquired the harassed one.

"He died!" she declared.                                        LAURIE, JR.

**213**

Elmer Smudgegump was an awful lush. One time he decided to quit drinking; so to prove to himself his strength of will, he passed by his favorite saloon that evening on his way home from work. Fifty feet past the saloon he stopped and said to himself—"Elmer, I'm proud of you! You're really a hero and have won a great moral victory! I didn't think you could do it, and I'm going to reward you! I'm going to take you right back to that saloon and—buy you a drink!"

FORD

**214**

Governor Bricker loves to tell stories, and this one rocked an audience recently in Cleveland.

Clancy was a Republican all of his life—so was his entire family. One night, about ten o'clock, he dashed into the Democratic Club.

"Hurry up and enroll me officially as a New Dealer!" he commanded.

"We appreciate the compliment," said the fellow in charge, "but we're closing right now. Can't you come here in the morning—what's your rush?"

"I had a fight with my family," explained Clancy, "and I want to do them a dirty trick!"          HERSHFIELD

**215**

Doyle was run over by one of those hit-and-run taxi drivers. As he lay in the street groaning, a cop rushed over to his side.

"Did you get the guy's number who hit you?" asked the cop.

"No, but I know him," moaned Doyle. "He's a barber!"

"What makes you think he's a barber?" asked the cop.

"He went over my face—twice!" replied Clancy.

LAURIE, JR.

## 216

An Italian owned a corner fruit store. Every day a dog would come by, steal an apple, and eat it. Finally, the Italian got tired of it, went to the Police Station and reported the dog to the Desk Sergeant. After hearing his story, the Desk Sergeant spoke.

"I can't do anything about that," he said. "It's probably a Police Dog!" FORD

## 217

A kind of goofy guy came home late one night and found his wife missing. The following morning, he discovered what happened, and called his bookkeeper into his office.

"When I first hired you as a bookkeeper you didn't know anything, but I didn't say anything," he reminded. "Then you started to steal stationery and stamps, and I didn't say anything. Then you gave away my secret prices to my competitors, and I didn't say anything! You stole money from the safe to play the races and never replaced it, and I didn't say anything! Now you've stolen my wife!" He drew a deep breath, looked darkly at the culprit, then added, "Listen, the next little thing you do—out you go!" HERSHFIELD

## 218

A hold-up man ordered a moron to fork over his dough but, instead, the moron started slugging away at him for dear life, with the hold-up man fighting back desperately. It was a terrific battle, starting on the sidewalk and winding up in the street. Finally the hold-up man tripped him, and the moron fell heavily. He quickly frisked his pockets, finding— sixty-five cents!

"Why did you put up a battle like that for a lousy sixty-five cents?" he asked in complete disgust.

"I thought you were going to find the thousand-dollar bill I've got hidden in my shoe!" gasped the moron.

LAURIE, JR.

**219**

A fellow, who had taken aboard a cargo of liquor, listed to the starboard as he left a night club early one morning. He staggered over to a waiting taxi and opened the door.

"I'm engaged!" informed the cab driver, curtly.

The drunk shook hands with him.

"I hope you will be very, very happy," he said.      FORD

**220**

In the great book *Cartoon Cavalcade* there's a gag about the first telephone. It shows a sketch of Clancy in his office holding the cord with the receiver dangling at the end of it. A fellow enters.

"What's wrong, Clancy?" he asks.

"The next time Finnegan tells me to hold the wire," rants Clancy, "he's coming here and do it himself!"

HERSHFIELD

**221**

Two women were walking along, conversing. On the corner, there was a man and a dog.

"Look at that dirty dog!" remarked one woman.

"How dare you talk that way about my husband!" snapped the other, indignantly. LAURIE, JR.

## 222

A schoolteacher was pointing out the difference between right and wrong to her little pupils, stressing the wickedness of stealing. She tried to illustrate her point.

"Now, children," she said, "if I put my hand in a man's coat pocket and took all of his money—what would I be?"

"You'd be his wife!" shouted a youngster. FORD

## 223

One winter morning, a man was lost in the Alps, so Maximilian, a big Saint Bernard dog, was sent out to search for him with a small keg of whiskey attached to his collar. At midnight, the Saint Bernard returned to headquarters and started barking.

"Woof! Woof!" he barked. "Maximilian reporting!"

"Did you find the man?" asked the keeper of the Saint Bernard.

"Yes," barked Maximilian.

"Was he conscious?" he inquired.

"When I found him," barked Maximilian, "he was cock-eyed. There's some bootlegging going on around here!"

HERSHFIELD

## 224

"My aunt is so absent-minded," remarked a man, "that the other day when she boiled some water to make tea, she put the kettle on the armchair and sat on the stove! We didn't know she was getting hot until she started—singing!"

LAURIE, JR.

**225**

An excited woman phoned the Police Station.

"Will you please send an officer immediately?" she pleaded. "There's a bad salesman sitting in the tree teasing my dog!"

FORD

**226**

Little Sammy was walking across a golf course and got hit on the head with a golf ball.

"I'll sue you in court for five hundred dollars!" he yelled at the golfer who hit him.

"I hollered 'Fore!'" alibied the golfer.

"I'll take it!" yelled Sammy.     HERSHFIELD

**227**

A fellow was invited to a friend's house for dinner. The host's son, little Willie, sat next to the guest. "I'll bet you can't do it! I'll bet you can't do it!" repeated little Willie.

"I can't do what?" asked the guest.

"My mother said that you were going to eat your head off tonight," explained little Willie, "and I'll bet you can't do it!"

LAURIE, JR.

**228**

Three colored gentlemen were playing poker. A hand was dealt, the pot was opened, and plenty of raising went on. Finally, the hands were called. "Ah win!" announced one fellow. "Ah has three aces an' a pair of queens!"

"Ah win!" declared the second fellow. "Ah has got three aces and a pair of queens!"

"None of you-all win!" informed the third one. "Ah does. Ah has got two deuces—an' a razor!"                    FORD

## 229

A moron entered a saloon five days straight with a carrot sticking out of each ear, and ordered a drink. But the bartender, who figured it was a gag, refused to ask the moron why he had the carrots in his ears. The sixth day, when the moron entered with a banana sticking out of each ear, the bartender's curiosity got the better of him.

"Why have you got those bananas sticking in your ears?" asked the bartender.

"I couldn't get any carrots!" explained the moron.

HERSHFIELD

## 230

A Scotchman's wife was very ill in bed. The only source of illumination in her room came from a small candle.

"I feel myself slipping," whispered the sick woman. "I'll probably die tonight."

"I've got to get back to work," declared the Scotchman, "but if you feel yourself slipping—be sure and blow out the candle!"                    LAURIE, JR.

## 231

After an operation, a man regained consciousness in his hospital room and found the shades drawn. He summoned enough strength to ask the doctor the reason.

"There's a fire across the street," explained the doctor,

"and I pulled down the shades for fear that if you saw the flames you'd think that the operation was a failure!"

FORD

## 232

Two old business partners, Max and Sam, were victims of overwork. They went to a doctor, who prescribed monkey glands to rejuvenate them. After taking his advice, Sam met a friend.

"I heard that you and Max got monkey glands now," remarked the friend. "How do you feel?"

"Marvelous!" enthused Sam. "I'm a regular athlete now! I play tennis, baseball, and swim like a champion!"

"How's your partner, Max?" inquired the friend.

"Confidentially," informed Sam, "I think they gave him old monkey glands, because all day long he hangs from a chandelier and eats peanuts!" HERSHFIELD

## 233

Jerry Doyle fell asleep and dreamed an angel appeared.

"I am going to give you just one wish," said the angel. "Whatever you wish will be granted!"

"I wish I could see a newspaper of 1946," wished Jerry, "so I could look up the market and see what stocks will be worth then. I could buy accordingly and make a lot of money!"

His wish was no sooner made than the newspaper appeared in his hand! He studied the stock-market quotations and made notes of different stocks he intended buying. Then he decided to peruse the rest of the paper. At the head of the Obituary column was the following notice: "Jerry Doyle—died today!"

LAURIE, JR.

**234**

A Scotchwoman, who ran a farm, had worn a hat so long that the neighbors decided to chip in and buy her a new one. They asked her what kind she preferred.

"A straw one," she replied, "because after I get through wearing it, it'll make a good meal for the cow!"        FORD

**235**

It was a hot summer day such as you often get in New York. As an old-clothes man ambled through the tenement district hollering, "Ole Clothes!" a woman on the sixth floor hailed him. Tired and weary, he trudged up the six floors carrying a big bag over his shoulders.

"Ole clothes?" he gasped, almost out of breath.

"No," answered the woman, then indicated a little crying boy and said, "Ain't you going to put him in that great big bag if he's a bad little boy?"        HERSHFIELD

**236**

A refugee arrived in New York. He couldn't speak or understand one word of English. Hungry, he went into a restaurant and sat at the counter. He didn't know how to order. The man who sat next to him ordered "Bean Soup," so the refugee repeated it when he was asked what he wanted. That's the only thing he knew how to order, with the result that for three weeks straight he had "Bean Soup" for break-fast, dinner, and supper! Naturally, he became a little tired of it and wanted a change; so he listened carefully in the restaurant, and one day heard a man order "Ham Sandwich."

The refugee memorized it, and when the waiter came for his order he said, "Ham Sandwich!"

"On white or rye?" asked the waiter.

Helpless and confused, the refugee answered, "Bean Soup!"

LAURIE, JR.

**237**

A fellow was arrested and taken to the Police Station.

"What's your name?" asked the Desk Sergeant.

"Size-Six McFadden," replied the man.

"That's a funny name, 'Size-Six,' " remarked the Desk Sergeant.

"That really isn't my name," declared McFadden. "As a matter of fact, my name is 'Six-And-Seven-Eighths!' "

"I don't get you," said the Sergeant, somewhat bewildered.

"Well, you see, when I was born, my parents didn't know what to call me," he explained, "so, they put a lot of names in a hat and by mistake my father pulled out the size of the hat!"

FORD

**238**

When Edward H. Little, President of Colgate-Palmolive-Peet Company, told me this story, I knew it would come handy for this program.

A glamorous, shapely, immaculately dressed female war correspondent went to the battlefront—in the thickest of the fray. Later, she returned to headquarters completely worn out, disheveled, mud all over her face, and gasping for breath!

"What happened?" asked a sentry in surprise.

"As soon as the battle started I got frightened and jumped into a wolf hole!" she said.

"You mean a fox hole," corrected the sentry.

"A fox may have dug it," she declared, "but there was a wolf in it!"                                    HERSHFIELD

## 239

A lawyer came to visit a new client. He introduced himself as follows:

"I represent Button, Button, Button, Button and Button. My name is Zipper—I replaced one of the Buttons!"

LAURIE, JR.

## 240

Chickens are really very ambitious—they'll hatch out anything! One of them sat on a cake of ice and hatched out two quarts of water. Another chicken dieted. Instead of eating grain, it ate sawdust—and laid twelve eggs. When they hatched, eleven of the baby chicks had wooden legs and the other one was—a woodpecker!                                    FORD

## 241

Sandy sold Jock his auto. The next day he was sorry he sold it, so he went to see Jock.

"I'll buy the car back from you, Jock," he said, "and give you fifty dollars profit!"

So, Jock sold him the car. The following day, he looked up Sandy.

"I'm sorry I sold the car back to you, Sandy," he said. "I'll give you seventy-five dollars profit for it!"

So, Jock bought the car back. The next day Sandy was sorry he sold it and bought it back again, giving Jock one hundred dollars profit! The day following, Jock came to buy it back but learned Sandy had sold it to MacPherson!

"You dope! Why did you sell it to a stranger?" reprimanded Jock, "especially when we were both making such
a wonderful living out of it!"          HERSHFIELD

## 242

An Irishman went to the beach and saw a little Jewish
fellow sitting on the sand.

"How's the water?" asked the Irishman.

"Lukewarm," replied the little Bronxman.

So, the Irishman went into the water but came out immediately, shivering, shaking and teeth chattering.

"W-w-what's the idea of t-t-telling me the w-w-water
was 'lukewarm'?" he demanded.

"Well," explained the innocent one, "it 'luked warm' to
me!"          LAURIE, JR.

## 243

A woman lost her thumb in a streetcar accident and sued
the streetcar company for five thousand dollars. In court,
the Judge asked her how she happened to place a valuation
of five thousand dollars on her lost thumb.

"Because, your Honor," explained the woman, "that's the
thumb I used to keep my husband under!"          FORD

## 244

A young man returned from college to his home on the
farm with new ideas and an entirely different viewpoint.
Everything was old-fashioned looking to him and he complained about it constantly.

"Look at that photograph on the wall of you sitting and

Mother standing," he sneered, "that's an awful old-fashioned thing!"

"With all of your education, Son, you've got plenty to learn," advised his Father. "That photograph was taken in the country just after I got through with a ten-mile hike and Mama got through horseback riding!" HERSHFIELD

## 245

On my last trip to Washington, I met George Marshall for lunch in the Shoreham Hotel, and he told me this one.

A Lieutenant decided to pay a surprise visit to the barracks and found everyone lounging around.

"Get up!" he commanded. "Throw that cigarette away! Wipe that smile off of your face!"

One man in particular appeared quite indifferent. This irked the Lieutenant.

"What outfit do you belong to?" demanded the Lieutenant, with rising anger.

"To the West Side Laundry," replied the man. "I just came for the bags!" LAURIE, JR.

## 246

This is Herbert Bayard Swope's favorite story.

A jealous wife searched her husband's pockets and found a card on which was scribbled—Marjorie Grey, Main 821. She confronted him with it.

"Marjorie Grey is just the name of a race horse I bet on," he explained.

"Oh, yeah? Well, explain what this 'Main' here means!" she demanded.

"Oh, that's the name of the street where my bookmaker lives!"

"821," she challenged. "Get out of that one—if you can!"

"Why, dear, those are the odds—eight to one!" he said, in hurt surprise.

He got away with it—temporarily. The following night when he came home he greeted his wife.

"Anything new today, honey?" he asked.

"Oh, nothing much," she replied, "except that your horse called up!"                                              FORD

## 247

A tall, well-built fellow went to the manager of a baseball team to apply for a position.

"I'm a great ballplayer," he said, talking very rapidly. "I'd be a great help to you because they're jerking able-bodied guys out of ball teams every day and I'm 4F and they wouldn't take me. I'm a great ball player! I can pitch! I can catch! I'm a swell outfielder! And in a pinch I can sell peanuts, popcorn, crackerjack, lemonade or scorecards!"

"You're nuts!" blurted the manager.

"That's why I'm in 4F!" he confessed.          HERSHFIELD

## 248

A husband and wife were walking down a country road—arguing.

"You and your relatives!" she said scornfully. "They come to the house, eat my food, drink my liquor and stay for weeks! I never saw such a bunch before!"

Just then they passed a jackass, and it brayed.

"One of your relatives," he said, indicating.

"Yes, my dear," agreed his spouse, "by marriage!"

LAURIE, JR.

**249**

Two kids were bragging about their ancestors, tossing in a few wild dreams, as youngsters usually do.

"Do you know that the King of England touched my great-great-grandfather on the head with a sword and made him a Duke?" boasted one.

"That's nothing," sneered the other. "An Indian Chief tapped my great-great-grandfather on the head with a tomahawk and made him an angel!"

FORD

**250**

Mr. Curtain Van de Water, late of Park Avenue, lost his entire fortune and was reduced to the bread line and free soup kitchen. Still very ultra, he was surprised when handed a bowl of beef stew.

"What, no menu?" he remarked. "No choice?"

"You get two choices here, Bud," growled the beef-stew dispenser, "take it or leave it!"

HERSHFIELD

**251**

Tommy Manville wowed a crowd one night at the Ritz with this story, which I think is one of the best I've heard.

An author was up until three o'clock in the morning working on a new book. His wife became very much annoyed and begged him to turn out the lights and go to bed.

"No, no, I can't!" replied the temperamental one. "I'm in a spot and I can't go to bed until I figure it out!"

"What is it?" asked his wife.

"The villain who's been buying the heroine clothes, dinners and nylon stockings has got her by the throat and is kissing her, swearing that she's the only one he loves! It's a dilemma and I've got to get her out of it!"

"How old is the heroine?" inquired the wife.

"Twenty-two years old!" he replied.

"Put out the lights and come to bed," demanded the wife. "She's old enough to get out of it herself!"          LAURIE, JR.

## 252

One day a little girl questioned her mother.

"Mama, do all fairy tales begin with—'once upon a time'?"

"No, my dear," replied her mother, "sometimes they begin with, 'Honey, I was detained at the office'!"          FORD

# 4

## CLOWN TABLE DISCUSSIONS

# FOOTBALL

FORD: Speaking about football, I know a coach on Pennsylvania—I know a coach on the B & O, too.

LAURIE, JR.: He knows an Indian coach—who has a caboose.

HERSHFIELD: Please don't mind if I avoid getting into a football discussion, because I won't have anything to do with pigskins.

LAURIE, JR.: I went to a football game once with a girl who was a telephone operator. She kept hollering to the players, "Hold the line, please! Hold the line, please!"

HERSHFIELD: I invited a friend who had never seen a football game before. We were about three-quarters of an hour late. "What's the score?" I asked the ticket seller. He said, "In the third half, nothing to nothing." My friend said, "We're lucky—we didn't miss a thing!"

LAURIE, JR.: I know a team that can't play in the Sugar Bowl because two of the fellows on the team have diabetes.

FORD: I know a fellow who was center—he had a guard on both sides of him. He was invited to play on the "All-Sing-Sing 'Eleven'." I know another fellow who was a drawback.

LAURIE, JR.: There is a team with all men on it—"Not-A-Dame!"

# THANKSGIVING

HERSHFIELD: I haven't a thing in my mind, but I have turkey in my stomach.

FORD: We had a twenty-two-pound turkey. It was stuffed with chestnuts—to remind me of this program!

LAURIE, JR.: A fellow went into a restaurant and remarked to the waiter, "It's depressing eating all alone on Thanksgiving Day." The waiter nodded, and said, "What will you have?" The morose chap said, "Bring me some turkey, and a few kind words, please." The waiter left and returned with the turkey. "Where are the few kind words?" asked the customer. The waiter replied, "Don't eat the turkey!"

FORD: After dinner at our house, we took the wishbone of the turkey and made wishes. I won, but I guess Hedy Lamarr doesn't believe in those things!

HERSHFIELD: November is a great month for the axe. As an example, take the politicians—many of them get axed!

FORD: A Lady Bountiful invited three little urchins to her home for Thanksgiving dinner. Before serving the kids, she asked each one what part of the bird he preferred. The first one said, "I'm going to be an aviator, so I'll take a wing." The second one said, "I'm going to be a musician, so I'll take the drumstick." When she asked the third kid what he wanted, he replied, "I'm a Dead End Kid, so—pass me up!"

# FLIES

HERSHFIELD: Did you see the newsreel pictures of Roosevelt, Churchill, and Stalin in Casablanca?

LAURIE, JR.: Casablanca—that's where the tsetse flies, isn't it?

FORD: You couldn't say there were any flies on them!

LAURIE, JR.: Speaking about flies, a man took his son to a restaurant one day and ordered soup for him. "Papa, look!" said the kid. "I've got a fly in my soup!" His father replied, "Drink it till you come to the fly, then ask for another bowl of soup!"

HERSHFIELD: There's another version of that story. A fellow in a restaurant complained about a fly in his soup, and the proprietor said, "I've got to congratulate you! All day long, the waiters were trying to catch that fly, but you, a total stranger—succeeded!"

FORD: The only flies I'm interested in are those caught by Brooklyn outfielders. However, there's still another version of the 'fly-in-the-soup' story—the one where the waiter brings in the soup and the customer says, "There's a fly in my soup," and the waiter replies, "Forget it! How much can a little fly drink?"

HERSHFIELD: That made the waiter the fly in the ointment!

## SINGING

LAURIE, JR.: One thing I know about singing is, that Harry Hershfield sings with his heart and soul—but he ought to try it with his voice some time.

FORD: I resent that, Joe. Harry knows six different songs, and no matter which one you ask him to sing, it always comes out, "If it's kissin' you are missin'."

LAURIE, JR.: Senator Ford is the original Long Island Sinatra. In fact, the Senator started in show business as a quartette —not as a whole quartette—just part of one. Their first job was to sing at a funeral. The poor man wasn't dead yet, so they sang until he died—which didn't take long!

FORD: My quartette was four people. Each one thought the other three were terrible and each one was three-quarters right, at that! But, confidentially, I was the only real good singer of the gang. By the way, do you know how a critic once described our singing?—I mean Hershfield, Laurie and myself—he said it sounded like three bees moaning in a horsehair sofa!

HERSHFIELD: We're better off if we sing, because we are men of note!

LAURIE, JR.: That's the voice of experience speaking!

HERSHFIELD: I received a letter from a fellow one time and he wrote, "Are you a duet or a trio with a spare?"

FORD: Did you answer, admitting you are the spare?

LAURIE, JR.: I doubt it, Senator. You know Harry's voice sounds like asthma—set to music!

FORD: Don't say that, Joe. Harry has one of those good voices —it's good for cooling clam chowder!

## NEW YEAR'S AND RESOLUTIONS

HERSHFIELD: Do you know why there's a shortage of paper? There are too many guys holding the bag, now!

FORD: Forget it. Tomorrow is January 1, A.D.—All Day.

LAURIE, JR.: I turned over a new leaf today—in my checkbook!

HERSHFIELD: Comes the resolution! I'm going to give up drinking—I gave up buying weeks ago!

LAURIE, JR.: All of my sisters made resolutions this morning. I think they're going to join the Daughters of the American Resolutions.

HERSHFIELD: A resolution is like medicine—when you forget to take it, you don't need it any more.

FORD: All the opponents of Joe Louis were like good resolutions—they were always carried out!

LAURIE, JR.: Just yesterday, I was talking to an old Scotchman. I said, "Are you going to buy a horn and help make it a noisy New Year's Eve?" He said, "No. There'll be plenty of noise around our house—I'm going to tear off a porous plaster from my son's chest!"

FORD: Last New Year's Eve I had a great time. I went out with a bunch of Indians. I knew they were Indians because they all had reservations!

## ORIGINALITY

HERSHFIELD: A lot of people claim originality in phrasing things. For instance, during the coal shortage last year, a friend of Mr. Ickes said, "There's no fuel like an old fuel!"

LAURIE, JR.: And, "you can fuel some of the people some of the time, but you can't fuel all of the people all of the time."

HERSHFIELD: You can fuel some of them part of the time— we know that!

FORD: There's nothing original about that routine because I did it in a radio show during the first world war. We used to have meatless Tuesday, too—remember?

HERSHFIELD: But there is someone who will always give you an argument, Senator. People imagine they've really never heard a phrase before and often think it's original with them. It even happened to the great Mark Twain. After claiming originality for something, it took him twenty years to find out his mistake—but he apologized publicly, when he discovered it.

FORD: I just thought of something which proves lack of originality. I've always had a great respect for the memory of John G. Whittier, because he thought of the idea of this program long before we did, when he wrote—"Up in the meadows, rich with corn!"

## LOOKS

LAURIE, JR.: I've received many letters lately from listeners who write in asking what Senator Ford looks like. I really don't know what to answer them!

HERSHFIELD: I'll tell you! Explain with a story. Just write that Senator Ford was ill not many days ago and a fellow who saw him met the Senator's wife on the street afterward. After salutations, he said, "Your husband looks like himself again." To which Mrs. Ford indignantly replied, "You have no right to insult him like that!"

LAURIE, JR.: For the unseen audience, I really would like to describe Senator Ford. Seriously, he looks like a contented halibut!

HERSHFIELD: He always looks like he's looking over his glasses so he won't wear them out!

LAURIE, JR.: But he has a nice, kind look—I didn't say what kind!

FORD: Are you fellows all through insulting me or just running out of material?

LAURIE, JR.: I've decided to follow Harry's advice and write. But instead of a story, I'm going to write a description of him, because I know he's a little bowlegged—they look like pliers. He's thin—a very thin man—in fact, as a kid, when he'd stand sideways in a schoolroom, the teacher would always say—"Mark him absent!"

## VAUDEVILLE

FORD: Harry Hershfield made a crack about me last week. He said that he was talking to a hermit and the hermit told him that he got used to being alone because he used to attend vaudeville houses that I played in. Well, I just want to say that Mr. Hershfield never played any big cities or even big towns—he played wide open spaces and crossroads. In fact, he played in spots that even Rand-McNally never heard of!

LAURIE, JR.: I get you—one had to look them up in a bird-seed catalogue!

HERSHFIELD: That's a funny thing—I didn't play vaudeville but, I'm still on this program—I can't understand that! By the way, Senator, this is no reflection on your education, but do you understand anything besides English?

FORD: I can't even understand English—when you speak it!

HERSHFIELD: That's all I wanted to know. "Hey, Joe!"

LAURIE, JR.: What?

HERSHFIELD: "Jela come pa, Senator Ford, mel a del mia?"

LAURIE, JR.: "Oh, pfels dey la mour mia ne see, Senator Ford!"

HERSHFIELD: "La, vier key outa, one hundred and forty on ze meter?"

LAURIE, JR.: "Avez vous—'We're not talking about you, Senator'—fif-tiee on the meter!"

HERSHFIELD: Joe! Wouldn't it be funny if what we're saying really meant something?

LAURIE, JR.: Doesn't it?

HERSHFIELD: "Le plue du!"

LAURIE, JR.: I do want to apologize to the Senator, though. Last week, I said that his face looked as if it was up in curlers. I didn't mean that.

HERSHFIELD: What do you mean, you didn't mean it?

LAURIE, JR.: Now that I look at it—I think it is!

FORD: "There were three men floating down a river on a marble slab"—Now, that's about as far as I'm going to go —I'll let you two fellows finish that gag, too!

## WEATHER

HERSHFIELD: For years the topic of conversation has been the weather. Even Mark Twain once said, "Everybody complains about it but nobody does anything about it." The Government has now permitted us to talk about the weather on the radio—if we wish.

LAURIE, JR.: Without taxing us?

HERSHFIELD: Fair enough!

LAURIE, JR.: Talking about the weather—one time in Texas, a dog was chasing a rabbit, and it was so hot—they both were walking!

HERSHFIELD: A fellow was comfortably seated in his living room, engrossed in a book. His wife said, "Close the window—it's cold outside!" Annoyed, he jumped up, slammed the window down and said, "Now, is it warmer outside?"

FORD: I like the Mexican weather report—Chile today—Hot tamale!

## JOKES

HERSHFIELD: Last night we were sitting around trying to remember the first joke we ever heard. I remember this one. A kid said to his father, "Say Pop, why is the Fourth of July?" The father asked, "Why?" The kid replied, " 'J'— is the first, 'U'—is the second, 'L'—is the third, and 'Y'— is the fourth of July!"

LAURIE, JR.: The first joke I remember was in Ward and Curren's act at old Tony Pastor's. Curren portrayed a judge, and a prisoner is brought before him. "What's the man charged with?" demanded the Judge. "Stealing nine bottles of beer!" blurted the cop. "Case dismissed!" bellowed the Judge. "You can't make a case out of nine bottles!"

FORD: The first joke I remember was the one my Aunt Ida told me when I was a little boy. She said, "There was a little boy who drew off his gloves, drew off his coat and drew off his shoes." "What was his name?" I asked. "Andrew," was her reply.

LAURIE, JR.: The first time I saw Weber and Fields they pulled this one. "I saw your sister." "Which sister?" "Ida, and oh, is she fat!" "I've got another sister—she's Lena!"

HERSHFIELD: Here's an oldie. A general said to his troops, "When the enemy gets within one thousand yards of our trenches, we're going to retreat. I'm a little lame, so I'm starting now!"

LAURIE, JR.: There's no such thing as an old joke. If you've never heard it—it's a new one. You never hear anyone say "break a joke to me"; they say, "crack a joke"—because jokes are indestructible.

HERSHFIELD: Here's proof of it. Some tourists were looking over the ruins of Rome. One remarked, "Rome wasn't built in a day." Another cracked, "Looks to me like it was!"

LAURIE, JR.: One of the oldest jokes in vaudeville was told me by Frank Bush. A beggar stopped a lady. "Will you please give ten cents to a blind man?" he pleaded. "Why, you can see with one eye," she said. "Then make it a nickel," compromised the beggar.

FORD: Here's one from 1826. An Irishman was riding a horse, and the horse started to kick up quite a bit. Finally, one of his legs got caught in the stirrup. The Irishman addressed the horse. "If you're going to get on," he said, "I'm going to get off!"

LAURIE, JR.: Here's one I heard over twenty-five years ago. Clancy died and his friend Finnegan went to pay his respects. In the parlor, Finnegan looked down at the casket and said to Mrs. Clancy, "He's still warm." She replied, "Hot or cold, he goes out in the morning!"

HERSHFIELD: Sam went to hear a faith-healer lecture. After, the faith-healer, who knew him, said, "Sam, how's your father?" "My father," informed Sam, "thinks he's sick." "You have the correct viewpoint," the faith-healer assured. A month later, Sam went to hear him lecture again. "How's your father?" inquired the faith-healer. "Oh," informed Sam, "he thinks he's dead! "

LAURIE, JR.: A circus came to town, and Timmie, a midget who worked in it, died. They laid him out in his second-floor room in the boarding house. One of his friends wanted to see him, so he asked permission of the woman who ran the place. "You can go up there, but don't forget to close the door after you come out!" she warned. "Why?" he asked, puzzled. "Because," she said, "the cat has had him down here three times already!"

# GEORGE WASHINGTON

HERSHFIELD: Tomorrow is the birthday of our first President, George Washington. He was well known for his keen sense of humor, and many of his quotations became famous.

LAURIE, JR.: He was the first one who tabooed eating spaghetti by saying, "Beware of foreign entanglements!"

HERSHFIELD: Many persons labor under the false impression that George Washington threw a silver dollar across the Potomac—it was the Rappahannock.

LAURIE, JR.: They call it the Potomac because they can't pronounce Rappahannock!

HERSHFIELD: Some people argue that George Washington couldn't throw a silver dollar across the Rappahannock—others argue that he could, because a dollar went further those days!

FORD: The truth of the matter is, that he really threw it to teach a couple of Scotchmen how to swim.

LAURIE, JR.: The first Scotchman that ever came across, I guess!

FORD: Of course, the most famous story about George Washington is the one about his cutting down the cherry tree and refusing to tell a lie. That's plausible, because a wife didn't ask questions those days. However, here's my version of the cherry tree—in rhyme:

> Small boy—sharp hatchet—
> Stern Dad—he'll catch it!
> Yes, Dad—I did,
> Can't lie—brave kid!

I never figured it required much bravery to tell the truth, especially when caught carrying an axe!

HERSHFIELD: Washington, Lincoln and Joe Laurie were all born in the same month!

LAURIE, JR.: That's right, Harry. You know, I don't believe the story about Lincoln being born in a log cabin, because he'd have been full of syrup if he was!

FORD: Lincoln was born in a log cabin, all right. In fact, he helped his father build it!

## STATESMEN

LAURIE, JR.: We shall try and talk about statesmen, which is nothing original these days!

FORD: Old-time Top Sergeants with a pair of dice!

HERSHFIELD: Will you stop rolling your bones?

FORD: Rolling them?—Rattling them!

LAURIE, JR.: The humor of candidates aspiring to become statesmen has often caused their defeat. As an illustration: One night a potential candidate was making a campaign speech before a vast crowd. A heckler shouted, "What are you going to do if you're elected?" "Young man," the candidate replied, "I'm worrying about what I'm going to do if I'm not elected!" Needless to add, he was not elected!

HERSHFIELD: When Cal Coolidge was President of the United States, his wife had a portrait painted of him as a surprise present and hung it in his study. He was scrutinizing it when a United States Senator entered the study. Coolidge indicated the portrait and the Senator gazed at it. Not a word was spoken for fifteen minutes. Then Coolidge said, "I think so, too!"

FORD: The man of few words, Cal Coolidge, had a caller one day. A Social Welfare worker wanted to see him. A friend bet her that the President wouldn't say three words to her, even if she did see him. So, he bet him. After being admitted to see the President, she was so thrilled she told him about her bet. "You lose," he said.

LAURIE, JR.: One day, Nicholas Longworth took me to a photographers' banquet at the Capitol. As we passed through the banquet hall, a gentleman called, "Sit down, Nick!" However, he continued on. I said, "Who was he, Mr. Longworth?" "A Congressman," informed Mr. Longworth. "I never like to sit at a banquet table with Congressmen." "Why?" I asked. "Because," he said, "it takes them so long to pass anything!"

HERSHFIELD: Speaking about Coolidge reminds me of Senator Borah, who was thought a rebel because he had the courage of his own convictions. One day, Mr. and Mrs. Coolidge were riding horseback throught a street in Washington. "Isn't that Senator Borah in the distance, riding horseback?" inquired Mrs. Coolidge. "It can't be him," assured the President. "The horse and rider are going in the same direction!"

FORD: As soon as the ink was dry on the Declaration of Independence, Benjamin Franklin said to his assembled colleagues, "We'd better all hang together or we'll hang separately!"

LAURIE, JR.: I believe the ex-Mayor of New York, Jimmie Walker, was not only one of the cleverest but was also the wittiest of statesmen. He once said, "All politicians have three hats—one they wear, one they throw in the ring, and one they talk through!"

## CHRISTMAS SHOPPING

FORD: Christmas shopping is really something. If you want to know what hard work is, try getting into a department store a week before Christmas! And it's no fun being shoved around. I went into the Toy Department yesterday and couldn't even play with the trains! The kids shoved me right away!

HERSHFIELD: I get a lot of fun in the five-and-ten-cent store with the trinket buyers. One of the stores has a sign that says—"No need for shoplifting at our prices!"

FORD: Many Christmas shoppers buy things they don't need with money they haven't earned to impress people they don't like!

HERSHFIELD: The first thing that turns green with envy in the spring is—Christmas jewelry!

LAURIE, JR.: Here's the way I figure: November runs into December, December runs into Christmas—and Christmas runs into money!

HERSHFIELD: I heard a fellow say to a clerk in a store, "I want to see a Christmas present for a woman." The clerk asked, "For your wife, or do you want to see something more expensive?"

FORD: What I enjoy around Christmas time are the secret family conferences about Papa's presents. Mama wants to buy Papa a shirt and the kids want to buy him a pair of socks—so it always ends up in a tie!

HERSHFIELD: One really hates to buy presents these days. Just last night, I heard a great commotion in my neighbor's house. They've got a little kid, and he was crying because his old man was socking him. I went next door and asked what it was all about. My neighbor said, "Can you imagine, after spending all day shopping for a present, I found an expensive bicycle, had it wrapped up in a box, and even carried it home in the subway. After I gave it to him, I tiptoed back into the room, and there was the bicycle in one corner, but he was in the other corner—playing with the box!"

FORD: A wife wanted a present for Christmas—a pet she didn't have to be bothered with. So her husband bought her—a Mexican Jumping Bean!

LAURIE: Early Christmas shopping often gets people into trouble. I know a fellow who was arrested for doing his Christmas shopping too early. He was caught in the store an hour before it opened!

HERSHFIELD: Three weeks before Christmas, a Scotchman shot

off his revolver and told his kid that Santa Claus committed suicide!

FORD: Last Christmas, I was sent a box of tobacco. It was so big, that when I opened it there were two auctioneers in it still arguing! But what I really wanted was a pair of ice skates with Sonja Henie on them!

## COMEDIENNES AND OTHER HUMORISTS

FORD: Florence Moore, who was really one of our greatest comediennes, went to the zoo one time. She returned home and said, "Oh, I saw a kangaroo with the cutest little wife! I know it was his wife, because it was in his pocket!"

HERSHFIELD: Speaking about comediennes, the first time I ever met Fanny Brice she was looking in the window of a fruit store that featured a new shipment of grapefruit. Incidentally, it was the first grapefruit Fanny had ever seen. "It wouldn't take many of them to make a dozen!" cracked Fanny.

LAURIE, JR.: George Burns came down to breakfast one morning and reached for the paper. "What's this, Gracie?" he asked Miss Allen. "Who tore this big hole in the middle of the paper?" "I did, Georgie Porgie," confessed Gracie. "Isn't that cute? Now you can talk to me and read the paper at the same time."

HERSHFIELD: This is Frank Fogarty's most famous story. Clancy came home for supper on a hot summer night and bawled out his wife. "Where's me supper!" he bellowed. "The likes of you talking that way," exclaimed his wife. "All day long I'm sweating over a hot stove and all day long you're in a nice, cool sewer!"

FORD: My favorite story that Fogarty used to tell was about the thug who held up an Irishman. "Your money or your life!" he demanded. "Take me life," pleaded the Irishman, "because I'm saving me money for me old age!"

HERSHFIELD: I like his story about the fellow who entered an Irishman's store that had two clocks on the wall—each with different time. "What's the idea of two clocks," he asked, "and each having different time?" "Well," informed the Irishman, "if they were the same time, what would be the need of two clocks?"

LAURIE, JR.: Immigration has affected American humor, because years ago the Irishman was typified as a hard worker but a belligerent person—the Italian was characterized by a grind organ and monkey—the Hebrew was typed by business gags.

HERSHFIELD: The famous monologist, Walter C. Kelly, otherwise known as the Virginia Judge, had a definite characterization. One of his stories that I like best was the one about the woman who said to the conductor, "Does this train stop at the Grand Central Station?" He replied, "If it doesn't, you'll see the dardnest crash you ever saw in your life!"

LAURIE, JR.: Frank Fogarty also told the one about the belligerent Irishman who would sooner fight than eat. One day, he got up and walked into a morgue. "I'll lick anyone in the house!" he shouted.

## TRAFFIC LIGHTS

FORD: When traffic lights were first used in New York they had a red light for "Stop," a green light for "Go," and an orange light for "Change." Some of the Hibernian cops wouldn't stand for the orange-colored light because every time they looked at it—they saw red!

HERSHFIELD: I heard an Irish cop complain because he didn't like the red above the green!

LAURIE, JR.: They say Mayor La Guardia took the masks off the traffic lights, but I can't figure how a little guy like that got up there!

HERSHFIELD: Before traffic lights were used, a fellow was having great difficulty in crossing Forty-second and Fifth Avenue because of the heavy traffic. He tried for an hour and couldn't make it. Suddenly he spotted a friend on the other side of the street. "Max!" he shouted. "How did you get over there?" "I was born on this side!" informed Max.

LAURIE, JR.: A fellow, all bandaged up, met a friend. "What happened to you?" asked the friend. "I passed a red light with my car and had an argument with a guy. One word led to another and he beat me up." "Why didn't you call a cop?" inquired the friend. "He was a cop!" confessed the damaged one.

## NAVY DAY

FORD: So today's Navy Day! Which reminds me that Cliff Gordon used to say, "Maybe we haven't got the finest Navy, but look at the fine oceans we've got!"

LAURIE, JR.: Mrs. Bloomberg met Mrs. Weinberg. "How's your son?" she asked. "He's in the Navy," replied Mrs. Weinberg. "On what ship?" inquired Mrs. Bloomberg. "There's two?" asked the surprised Mrs. Weinberg.

HERSHFIELD: Clancy was so anxious to cross the Atlantic Ocean that he couldn't wait for a ship and decided to swim. Halfway across, he got frightened and he swam back!

LAURIE, JR.: An officer was questioning a Navy recruit. "If you were on duty and saw a huge battleship coming toward you over the hill, what would you do?" "I'd stop drinking!" confessed the recruit.

HERSHFIELD: A couple of sailors on shore leave passed a Picture Theater. On the marquee was: "Errol Flynn in 'The Pursuit of the North.'" "He's chasing everything, isn't he?" remarked one.

FORD: A Marine met a sailor in the subway. "Can you tell me how to get to Queens?" he asked. "You Marines are all alike," cracked the sailor. "I'm looking for one queen and you want two!"

HERSHFIELD: I know a fellow who calls his wife a Marine. Every time they have a fight, she's the first to land!

## VACATIONS AND HOLLYWOOD

FORD: It was wonderful over the week-end up in the country where I live, and I don't remember when I enjoyed a vacation more. Mentioning vacations, reminds me of the story of the fellow who died, went to Heaven and was met at the pearly gates by Saint Peter. "Where did you come from?" asked Saint Peter. "From Hollywood," answered the spook. "Well," said Saint Peter, "you can come in but—I don't think you'll like it here!"

HERSHFIELD: I've been to Hollywood four times and the last three times was my own fault!

LAURIE, JR.: The first time was their fault!

FORD: And if you were getting paid, it wasn't a vacation for them, either!

LAURIE, JR.: I like California for a vacation, and especially Hollywood. The only difference between Hollywood and New York is—in New York when they wear pants, they mean it!

HERSHFIELD: I'm considered a big-shot out on the coast. In fact, two California cities are fighting over me—Los Angeles insists that I was born in San Francisco and San Francisco insists I was born in Los Angeles.

LAURIE, JR.: For years I used to take my wife to Coney Island every day for a vacation, so just the other evening she said, "Look, Joe. Instead of taking me one thousand times to Coney Island, take me one time to the Thousand Islands!"

FORD: I'm so busy these days that when you see me take a deep breath—that's my vacation!

HERSHFIELD: When I hear about vacations, I always think of the Irishman who was asked if he liked to summer in the country. "Faith, no!" he replied. "I like to simmer in the city!"

LAURIE, JR.: That's like the girl who stopped to drop a coin in a beggar's tin cup. The coin dropped through and disappeared in the gutter. "Do you know you have a hole in your tin cup?" she asked. "Yeah," he declared, "I'm on my vacation this week!"

## VICTORY GARDENS

LAURIE, JR.: I like the idea of planting Victory Gardens, but I think people should grow vegetables that are characteristic of their business. For instance, plumbers should grow leek—cops should grow beets—jewelers, carrots, and jockeys, horseradish!

FORD: Up in my home town, Elmer Smudgegunk started a Victory Garden. He took cucumber seeds and turned them inside out before planting them. I asked him why he turned them inside out. "Because," he said, "I want to grow cucumbers with dimples instead of warts!"

HERSHFIELD: Which reminds me of ex-President Herbert Hoover's famous speech—words to the effect that if he was not elected, grass would grow in the city streets. Then came—Victory Gardens!

FORD: "How is your Victory Garden doing?" asked a friend. "Swell," informed the businessman. "I've got potatoes, cabbages, tomatoes and everything!" "I'll bet you don't even know how to pick a tomato," kidded his friend. "Oh, no? Did you ever see my wife?" was the retort.

HERSHFIELD: Last spring, a friend of mine, who knew absolutely nothing about gardens, received several packages of seeds from his Congressman. He planted them and a profusion of varicolored flowers blossomed, but he didn't know one from another. One day, a fellow from New York came to visit him and saw his beautiful garden. Strange as it may sound, he had to identify each flower for him. "What makes you such an expert with flowers?" asked the amateur gardener. "And how could you tell that was a pansy?" "I'm in the millinery business," exclaimed the Easterner.

LAURIE, JR.: A little old lady decided to have some flowers planted on either side of her garage, so she went into consultation with her gardener, who happened to be an Irishman. "I think we'll plant the spitunias on this side here," she said. "What would you suggest planting on the other side?" "Well, Ma'am," he mused, "if you're going to plant the spitunias there—I'd plant the cuspidors here!"

## SONG TITLES

LAURIE, JR.: I was just thinking of the days in Vaudeville when the old-time comedians would come out on the stage and score laughs with song titles. The formula was this: "Ladies and Gentlemen! I will now sing a little song entitled 'It wasn't the cough that carried him off, it's the coffin they carried him off in'!"

HERSHFIELD: Remember the song title "Everyone Has Someone, Darling, But I Only Have You"?

FORD: And the volcano song title "Lava, Come Back To Me!"

HERSHFIELD: Ben Welsh, the famous comedian, had a famous song title—"I'd Give Ten Thousand Dollars, To Be A Millionaire!"

FORD: Nat Wills, the tramp comic, had one, too—"Will Spearmint Keep Its Flavor On The Bedpost Overnight?"

LAURIE, JR.: Jimmy Conlin's was—"Father Get the Hammer —There's A Fly On Baby's Head!"

FORD: Lew Dockstader, the famous Minstrel Man, had one— "When You're Sick, They Bring You Fruit And Sit On The Bed And Eat It!"

HERSHFIELD: Morton and Moore had one—"Keep Off Of My Pool Table, You Are Wearing Off The Green!"

## SPRING

LAURIE, JR.: Spring is in the air! I know it, because just this morning I read an ad in a Florida paper and it said: Crow Flying North. Will Take Two Robins—Share Expenses!

FORD: With me, spring means baseball! I'm going to make an effort to revolutionize the game and speed it up. Instead of running from Home Plate to First Base, they ought to run from Home Plate to Third Base—then you can throw out a long fly!

HERSHFIELD: With me, spring means "Amour" and poetry!

LAURIE, JR.: Amour—that's a Ham, isn't it?—Amour Ham!

FORD: About four hundred points!

HERSHFIELD: Spring inspires thoughts of love, which reminds me of the story of Max, a poet who never dreamed that his pal was his wife's secret lover. "I'm a great artist," he admitted to his pal. "I create beautiful poetry like this— 'Roses are red—Violets are Blue—You're not me—And I'm not you'!" He paused. "What do you think of that?" he asked. "Marvelous," remarked the lover; "in fact, it's sensational!" Elated, Max said, "Can you originate poetry?" "Certainly," assured the lover. "Get this—'Roses are red— Violets are blue. You know, Max, I'm in love with your wife?" Annoyed, the temperamental poet said, "You darn fool—that doesn't rhyme!"

LAURIE, JR.: Speaking of spring, I thought I saw a robin this morning, but it turned out to be a sparrow with red underwear on!

FORD: Harry's poetic endeavor brings to my mind a personal experience one day in spring some years ago:

> I'll never forget her trim silhouette
> As she stood on the beach at my side.
> I'll always recall her figure tall,
> As she gazed at the incoming tide;
> I can still see her there
> As I said, "Maiden fair,
> Believe me, you're some nifty squaw!"
> I still count the stars, and I still sport the scars
> And I still feel the sock on the jaw!

## WITTY RETORTS

LAURIE, JR.: Gene Fowler, the famous author of *The Great Mouthpiece* and other well-known books, is in the top flight when it comes to witty retorts. One night, at a dinner party, a terrible pest addressed him. "You're Gene Fowler, aren't you?" he asked. "I am," confessed Gene. "I want to tell you who I am," said the pest. "Please don't," pleaded Gene. "Let me dislike you incognito!"

FORD: Ilka Chase is pretty quick on the trigger, too, when it comes to witty retorts. One day, a Hollywood ham said, "Miss Chase, when I was a young man my father offered me five thousand dollars if I wouldn't become an actor!" "What did you do with the money?" shot back Ilka.

HERSHFIELD: Everyone knows how good George Bernard Shaw is on pulling "nifties," but they are usually of the acid variety. One evening he attended a swank party. After an hour or so, the hostess, a dowager type, finally got around to speak to him. "Are you enjoying yourself, Mr. Shaw?" she gushed in a solicitous manner. "Yes," assured the bearded one, "and that's the only thing I'm enjoying!"

FORD: When Eugene Field worked for the old Denver *Post* he had occasion to attend a banquet in honor of a local politician who was feared, but not liked. The politician cornered him. "Have you ever seen me before, Mr. Field?" the politician asked, with meaning. "Yes," answered Field, "I was standing in front of this building when an empty cab drove up and you stepped out!"

LAURIE, JR.: An actor stopped the late Willie Collier, Sr., on the street and said, "Guess how much I made last year?" "Half!" snapped Collier.

# CAN YOU TOP THIS?

HERSHFIELD: An out-of-town newspaperman was a guest of mine, so to impress him I took him to the opening of a new show. It was a very bad show. After the second act I said, "How do you like the show?" "I wish I had taken you to it instead!" he replied.

FORD: John Barrymore was better than a green hand at handing out witty retorts. One time a man walked up to him and said, "Mr. Barrymore, which one of the Barrymores are you?" "Ethel!" answered John.

## "BUGS" BAER

HERSHFIELD: In my opinion, "Bugs" Baer is the greatest humorist alive. More comedians have used his material than that of any other humorist in the world. Which reminds me of an appropriate story. One time he went to a vaudeville show, and as different comedians came out and did their routines "Bugs" jotted them down. A friend sitting next to him remarked, "What are you doing?" "Collecting my thoughts," informed the mighty "Bugs."

LAURIE, JR.: "Bugs" is the one who originated "Alimony is like buying oats for a dead horse!" and thousands of other similes. One I especially like is—"As dizzy as a pickpocket with three arms who has an extravagant family!"

FORD: One Saturday afternoon "Bugs" was at his radio listening to a football game. That was the year the star of the team ran in the wrong direction. "He's just a backward student, that's all," explained "Bugs."

HERSHFIELD: Describing a very tough neighborhood, "Bugs" wrote, "It's so tough there, canaries sing bass!"

## WILSON MIZNER

LAURIE, JR.: One of the greatest wits of all times was the late Wilson Mizner. He was a great playwright, too. One of his best was *The Deep Purple*, which he wrote in collaboration with Paul Armstrong. It opened in London and was a tremendous hit. After the opening performance, the audience stood up en masse and shouted "Author! Author!" Mizner was forced to leave the wings and come out on the stage. He took a bow, then said, "This stage isn't big enough to hold all the authors of this play!"

FORD: One night in a famous old restaurant called "Jacks," a drunk thought Mizner was flirting with his girl; so in a pugnacious mood, he staggered over to his table. "Listen, mug!" he said, breathing one-hundred-proof whiskey in his face. "I'm going to punch you in the nose!" Mizner, who was over six-foot tall and quite a scrapper himself, got a full load of the drunk's breath, recovered and cracked, "You can't punch me in the nose, but your breath can start a windmill in a Dutch landscape!"

HERSHFIELD: A pest, who insisted upon being a wisecracker but was a complete failure at it, got a job on the air as a radio commentator. His one ambition was to be complimented by Mizner, so before his maiden broadcast he begged Wilson to listen, assuring him he would get plenty of laughs. That night Mizner listened. The next day the self-satisfied broadcaster collared him. "How did you like it?" he asked. "If you don't get off the air," warned Mizner, "I'll stop breathing!"

LAURIE, JR.: When President Cal Coolidge died, a friend dashed into Mizner's home and said, "Coolidge is dead!" "How can you tell?" cracked Mizner.

FORD: In his later years, Mizner went to Hollywood and wrote for the movies. He gave that up and bought an interest in the Brown Derby Restaurant in Hollywood. One day an interviewer asked him why he gave up writing for motion pictures to go into the restaurant business. "Because," informed Mizner, "I found out it was easier to get a steak into a producer's head than an idea!"

HERSHFIELD: One time Mizner had an experience with a Hollywood producer that caused him to speak his mind in no uncertain terms. The producer, who was no mental giant, to say the least, had rejected three great stories which had proven hits as plays on Broadway, but the pin-head producer wasn't aware of it. Finally, in complete disgust, Mizner cracked, "Young man, a demitasse cup would fit over your head like a sun bonnet!"

LAURIE, JR.: I like the one Wilson Mizner pulled in the old days when he was doing the best he could with the tools he had in Alaska. Those were the Gold Rush days. A confidence man came to Mizner's gambling joint to cash a check which Wilson suspected needed vulcanizing. The "con" man gave out with some fast talk, but Mizner had his number and refused to cash the check. "What kind of a guy do you think I am?" asked the "con" man. "You're the kind of a guy who would steal a hot stove and come back for the smoke!" replied Mizner.

HERSHFIELD: Mizner was in the witness chair one day and kept up a steady stream of gab, especially when the Judge was talking. Exasperated, the Judge grabbed his gavel, pounded with it, then stared menacingly at Mizner. "Are you trying to show your contempt of court?" he bellowed. "No," assured Mizner. "I'm trying to conceal it!"

FORD: One time Grant Clark, the famous lyricist and a great

pal of Mizner, came to Hollywood to visit him. They hadn't seen each other in many months, and Clark, who was very ill and sickly looking, said, "How do I look, Bill?" "I can get a two-hundred-dollar advance on you from any undertaker!" summarized Mizner.

## JOE FRISCO

HERSHFIELD: Joe Frisco, the famous entertainer, is quite a character and a well-known wit. Although he stutters, he socks over his lines. Always an independent fellow in business, Joe suffered because of it on numerous occasions, invariably refusing to cut his salary. One time a booking agent met him and said, "Frisco, I may have an engagement for you in a Chicago café. I'll call you up later. Will you be home?" "C-c-call me up," said Frisco, "b-b-but if y-y-you hear the re-re-receiver come off, and then you don't hear n-n-nothing for a long time—d-d-don't hang up —it's me!"

LAURIE, JR.: One day in the old Friars Club, Burton Holmes was relating one of his experiences to an interested group, including Frisco. This particular experience was with Indians. "Do you know that Indians never laugh?" remarked Mr. Holmes. Joe Frisco interrupted, "Oh, no?" he stuttered. "W-w-what's the matter with M-M-Minnie H-H-Ha-Ha?"

FORD: Frisco went into a restaurant one day and started to order. "I want s-s-some, s-s-some——" Before he could get the words out of his mouth, a cat jumped up on his lap!

LAURIE, JR.: I like the story about Frisco's first experience at a society tea room. He escorted a couple of Park Avenue debs. After the tea and cakes, Frisco was handed a bill for ten dollars. "H-h-hey, lady," he called to the waitress, "w-w-what did you put in the t-t-tea—platinum?"

HERSHFIELD: The time the banks were closing, Frisco was one of the first in line. Just as he reached the cashier's window, it was closed. "W-w-wait a minute!" he called. "W-w-where are you going?" "We're closing the bank temporarily," informed the cashier, curtly. Frisco looked around and said, "It's a long, long way to T-t-temporary!"

## BONERS

HERSHFIELD: The boner of all boner gags, and the one I like most, is the one about the two fellows who went into a ritzy resaurant for the first time. When the meal was finished, the waiter brought each a finger bowl. "What's this for?" asked one. "To wash your fingers," informed the waiter. The other fellow looked annoyed, then said to his friend, "If you didn't ask foolish questions, you wouldn't get foolish answers!"

LAURIE, JR.: Here's a boner that handed me a laugh today. An old lady got on a packed Fifth Avenue Bus. The conductor was very polite and concerned about her being unable to find a seat. After looking around, he said, "I'd like to give you a seat, Madam, but all of the empty ones are full!"

FORD: Kids often pull boners, and especially in schoolrooms. One kid said that *Bambi* was a story of Babe Ruth, and another kid said a "fjord" was a Swedish automobile!

LAURIE, JR.: A college professor lost his glasses and said, "I've got to find them before I can look for them!"

FORD: A woman came out of a chiropodist's office with a large package wrapped in brown paper. She was muttering

to herself. "Fine chiropodist," she said. "He don't know
how to stuff a dog!"

## CHRISTMAS PRESENTS

LAURIE, JR.: I want to thank you for that wallet you gave me
for Christmas, Senator. If you don't mind, I'll add two
and a half dollars and get a three-dollar one.

FORD: That's the best imitation leather wallet I could find.
Incidentally, that was a darb of a necktie you sent me!

LAURIE, JR.: Did you like it?

FORD: Yes. But why was it all wet when I received it?

LAURIE, JR.: The fellow didn't have an umbrella over his
pushcart. Say, Harry! Did you get that check I sent you?

HERSHFIELD: I got it twice—once from you and once from
the bank!

LAURIE, JR.: The money may not be there, but the spirit is.

HERSHFIELD: Which reminds me—did you get the liquor I
sent you?

LAURIE, JR.: Who did you send it with?

HERSHFIELD: With the doorman—the fellow with the big red
nose.

LAURIE, JR.: That's like sending lettuce leaves with a rabbit!

## WIT AND HUMOR

LAURIE, JR.: The Senator, Pat O'Brien of Hollywood, and
others were discussing wit and humor at the Lambs Club
the other night. I remarked that one of the wittiest things
I ever remember was the time Ring Lardner received an
invitation to appear at a banquet which he could not attend.
So he sent the Committee the following wire: "Sorry, children's night out, and I must stay home with the nurse!"

HERSHFIELD: A bore was making a long-winded speech at a banquet, and after gabbing for over an hour he said, "I'm sorry, Ladies and Gentlemen, but I haven't got my watch with me." A fellow hollered, "There's a calendar in back of you!"

FORD: Talking about wit and humor reminds me of a sign that was tacked on the Lambs Club Bulletin Board. It read: Lost—one cuff link. Owner will buy it or sell other one!

LAURIE, JR.: That isn't wit or humor—that's business! One night I went to a circus and after the performance visited a couple of midgets that I knew. They were the proud parents of a new little baby. As the father showed the baby to me, he cracked, "A sparrow brought him!"

HERSHFIELD: They say the way to make an Englishman laugh in his old age is to tell him a funny story when he's a boy!

LAURIE, JR.: That's why they do not allow any funny pictures to be shown in England on Saturday—so they won't laugh in church on Sunday!

HERSHFIELD: They don't say "Mickey the Mouse" in England —they call it—"Michael the Rodent"!

FORD: An Englishman took his son to an Art Museum, and when he came to the statue of Venus de Milo he said, "You see, my son, that's what comes of biting your nails!"

LAURIE, JR.: An English Colonel was at his club reading a newspaper. A younger member approached him. "Sorry to disturb you, Colonel," he said, "but I just learned that you buried your wife last week." "Of course, of course," said the Colonel, "I had to, you know—she was dead!"

## HUMOR ON TOMBSTONES

FORD: The other evening we were talking about humor and the unexpected places one finds it. As an example, epitaphs on tombstones. Now here's an old one: "Here lies the body of Mary O'Toole—She borrowed a feather to tickle a mule!"

HERSHFIELD: I remember one epitaph: "Here lies the body of Jake Ginsberg—if not, notify Bloomberg, the undertaker—immediately!"

LAURIE, JR.: A fellow had ten operations and finally died. A monument was placed over his grave bearing the following epitaph: "Pop has gone to join his appendix and tonsils—This is on him!"

HERSHFIELD: Groucho Marx told me his epitaph is going to be —"Here lies the body of Groucho Marx—who?"

FORD: Here's an epitaph I'd like to see: "Here lies the body of Hirohito, buried under ground, six feet-o!"

## CRITICS' HUMOR

FORD: Last week, Kelcey Allen, Ward Moorehouse, Len Liebling and I were discussing the strange and unusual type of humor dished out by critics. They say a critic is a kibitzer, with a side-kick.

LAURIE, JR.: I like the nifty that Walter Winchell pulled after sitting through a bad performance of a new show. Here's how he added it up: "Those without sin shall stone the first cast."

FORD: Guy Standing, who later was titled, made the mistake of trying to play Hamlet one time. Alan Dale saw the opening night's performance and wrote: "I still think Hamlet is a great play, not with standing!"

HERSHFIELD: Over the marquee of a motion-picture theater was the title of the picture and under it, four big stars. I went to see it and it really was so poor that I went to see the manager. "Who gave that picture four stars?" I asked. "I did," confessed the self-appointed critic. "I like it!"

FORD: Bob Fitzsimmons, one-time heavyweight champion of the world, was a fine specimen of manhood. One time he joined the *Uncle Tom's Cabin* troop, playing the leading role. They opened in a small western town. After the performance, a critic wrote: "Fitzsimmons was anatomically great, but Uncle Tomically he was terrible!"

## WIRES AND RATIONING

FORD: As everyone knows, during the war the telegraph companies refused to send congratulatory wires. Which reminds me of the famous wire a wife sent to her husband: "Just had twins—more by mail!"

LAURIE, JR.: Harry Lauder sent us a wire one time. It said: "Congratulations!—what more can I say in ten words!"

HERSHFIELD: It all comes under the heading of rationing of words. Which reminds me of my brilliant Aunt. I said to her, "If the war keeps on we may have to ration bread." She replied, "All right, then I'll eat toast!"

LAURIE, JR.: Talking about rationing, there's a very expensive restaurant in the Fifties which has this sign in the window: "Meals—Two dollars up." One day a fellow went in and said, "I want one of your two-dollar meals." The waitress asked, "On rye or white?"

# HOW THE "CAN YOU TOP THESE?" STORIES AND JOKES SCORED ON THE LAUGH METER

| | | | | | | | | | |
|---|---|---|---|---|---|---|---|---|---|
| 1 | 1000 | 32 | 1000 | 63 | 1000 | 94 | 700 | 125 | 950 |
| 2 | 1000 | 33 | 1000 | 64 | 800 | 95 | 1000 | 126 | 900 |
| 3 | 1000 | 34 | 900 | 65 | 1000 | 96 | 700 | 127 | 1000 |
| 4 | 1000 | 35 | 1000 | 66 | 1000 | 97 | 600 | 128 | 1000 |
| 5 | 1000 | 36 | 1000 | 67 | 600 | 98 | 1000 | 129 | 1000 |
| 6 | 1000 | 37 | 1000 | 68 | 1000 | 99 | 1000 | 130 | 1000 |
| 7 | 1000 | 38 | 1000 | 69 | 1000 | 100 | 600 | 131 | 950 |
| 8 | 1000 | 39 | 900 | 70 | 750 | 101 | 1000 | 132 | 1000 |
| 9 | 750 | 40 | 800 | 71 | 800 | 102 | 1000 | 133 | 1000 |
| 10 | 1000 | 41 | 1000 | 72 | 1000 | 103 | 1000 | 134 | 950 |
| 11 | 800 | 42 | 1000 | 73 | 700 | 104 | 1000 | 135 | 900 |
| 12 | 1000 | 43 | 1000 | 74 | 1000 | 105 | 1000 | 136 | 1000 |
| 13 | 1000 | 44 | 1000 | 75 | 1000 | 106 | 1000 | 137 | 950 |
| 14 | 800 | 45 | 1000 | 76 | 600 | 107 | 1000 | 138 | 900 |
| 15 | 800 | 46 | 1000 | 77 | 1000 | 108 | 1000 | 139 | 850 |
| 16 | 800 | 47 | 1000 | 78 | 1000 | 109 | 1000 | 140 | 900 |
| 17 | 1000 | 48 | 1000 | 79 | 1000 | 110 | 1000 | 141 | 1000 |
| 18 | 1000 | 49 | 1000 | 80 | 900 | 111 | 900 | 142 | 1000 |
| 19 | 1000 | 50 | 600 | 81 | 1000 | 112 | 950 | 143 | 900 |
| 20 | 1000 | 51 | 750 | 82 | 600 | 113 | 1000 | 144 | 950 |
| 21 | 1000 | 52 | 900 | 83 | 1000 | 114 | 950 | 145 | 1000 |
| 22 | 1000 | 53 | 1000 | 84 | 1000 | 115 | 900 | 146 | 1000 |
| 23 | 850 | 54 | 1000 | 85 | 850 | 116 | 1000 | 147 | 1000 |
| 24 | 900 | 55 | 1000 | 86 | 800 | 117 | 1000 | 148 | 1000 |
| 25 | 1000 | 56 | 600 | 87 | 700 | 118 | 1000 | 149 | 900 |
| 26 | 1000 | 57 | 1000 | 88 | 1000 | 119 | 950 | 150 | 950 |
| 27 | 1000 | 58 | 600 | 89 | 1000 | 120 | 950 | 151 | 1000 |
| 28 | 1000 | 59 | 750 | 90 | 950 | 121 | 900 | 152 | 900 |
| 29 | 700 | 60 | 1000 | 91 | 1000 | 122 | 1000 | 153 | 1000 |
| 30 | 1000 | 61 | 1000 | 92 | 1000 | 123 | 1000 | 154 | 850 |
| 31 | 1000 | 62 | 1000 | 93 | 1000 | 124 | 1000 | 155 | 900 |

# HOW THE "CAN YOU TOP THESE?" STORIES AND JOKES SCORED ON THE LAUGH METER—*Cont'd*

| | | | | | | | | | |
|---|---|---|---|---|---|---|---|---|---|
| 156 | 1000 | 175 | 1000 | 194 | 1000 | 213 | 1000 | 233 | 950 |
| 157 | 800 | 176 | 1000 | 195 | 1000 | 214 | 1000 | 234 | 850 |
| 158 | 1000 | 177 | 900 | 196 | 850 | 215 | 950 | 235 | 1000 |
| 159 | 1000 | 178 | 850 | 197 | 800 | 216 | 850 | 236 | 1000 |
| 160 | 1000 | 179 | 1000 | 198 | 950 | 217 | 1000 | 237 | 1000 |
| 161 | 1000 | 180 | 1000 | 199 | 1000 | 218 | 1000 | 238 | 1000 |
| 162 | 1000 | 181 | 1000 | 200 | 1000 | 219 | 1000 | 239 | 1000 |
| 163 | 1000 | 182 | 1000 | 201 | 1000 | 220 | 850 | 240 | 1000 |
| 164 | 900 | 183 | 850 | 202 | 1000 | 221 | 950 | 241 | 900 |
| 165 | 850 | 184 | 900 | 203 | 900 | 222 | 1000 | 242 | 900 |
| 166 | 1000 | 185 | 850 | 204 | 1000 | 223 | 1000 | 243 | 850 |
| 167 | 1000 | 186 | 1000 | 205 | 1000 | 224 | 1000 | 244 | 950 |
| 168 | 800 | 187 | 1000 | 206 | 850 | 225 | 1000 | 245 | 1000 |
| 169 | 1000 | 188 | 1000 | 207 | 1000 | 226 | 1000 | 246 | 1000 |
| 170 | 1000 | 189 | 900 | 208 | 1000 | 227 | 1000 | 247 | 1000 |
| 171 | 1000 | 190 | 1000 | 209 | 800 | 228 | 1000 | 248 | 950 |
| 172 | 800 | 191 | 1000 | 210 | 900 | 229 | 1000 | 249 | 1000 |
| 173 | 1000 | 192 | 1000 | 211 | 1000 | 230 | 900 | 250 | 850 |
| 174 | 1000 | 193 | 1000 | 212 | 1000 | 231 | 950 | 251 | 1000 |
| | | | | | | 232 | 1000 | 252 | 1000 |

# INDEX

235